Macroeconomics of Western Balkans in the Context of the Global Work and Business Environment

Macroeconomics of Western Balkans in the Context of the Global Work and Business Environment

Mirjana Radović-Marković
Business Academy University

Borislav Đukanović
University of Donja Gorica

INFORMATION AGE PUBLISHING, INC.
Charlotte, NC • www.infoagepub.com

Library of Congress Cataloging-in-Publication Data

CIP record for this book is available from the Library of Congress
http://www.loc.gov

ISBNs: 978-1-64802-914-1 (Paperback)

        978-1-64802-915-8 (Hardcover)

        978-1-64802-916-5 (ebook)

Printed in the United States of America

CONTENTS

PREFACE

New information and communication technologies have created a new world of work in which large international institutions stimulate competition without restrictions on the global labor market through network platforms. This offers for a "virtual migration" similar economic benefits as classic physical migration. It is assumed that the underdeveloped regions of Africa and especially Southeast Asia, which have already progressed very quickly (e.g., Pakistan), will receive special benefits from these "virtual migrations." Namely, it is known that those who have the highest unemployment rates, would get the greatest benefits.

Western Balkan countries will also need to cope with the new social and economic conditions on the global labor market. In this way, they will not only reduce unemployment rate, but also the gap with developed countries.

This study represents a significantly expanded continuation of the study on work from home (Radović-Marković et al., 2021). Unlike previous research in the case of Serbia, this one cover three more countries in the Western Balkans such as BiH, Montenegro and Northern Macedonia. We did this with an aim to compare results based on the application of the same research instruments at the regional level. In this way, we indirectly wanted to examine the validity and reliability of our instruments that we constructed by ourselves.

Considering four countries in the region, we were able to examine the similarities and differences of work from home. Finally, unlike the previous

Macroeconomics of Western Balkans in the Context of the Global Work and Business Environment, pp. ix–x
Copyright © 2022 by Information Age Publishing
www.infoagepub.com

one, this study is based on a more extensive presentation of the results. We expect that this book will make a significant contribution to the issue and serve in further research.

July 30, 2021

Mirjana Radović-Marković
Borislav Đjukanović

REFERENCE

Radović-Marković, M., Đjukanović, B., Marković, D., & Dragojević, A. (2021). *Entrepreneurship and work in the gig economy: The case of the Western Balkans.* Routledge.

PART I

THE MACROECONOMIC ENVIRONMENT IN THE WESTERN BALKANS COUNTRIES

CHAPTER 1

MACROECONOMIC ENVIRONMENT

Mirjana Radović-Marković

Strengthening the role of governance, education and social inclusion is of great importance to improving countries' capacity for innovation, a stable financial environment, the successful implementation of broadly set reforms and the establishment of a macroeconomic environment that supports private sector activities.

The macroeconomic environment in the Western Balkans countries is based on the progress of the market economy and the development of the private sector. However, in this region, the reform momentum has slowed in many countries, which has been reflected in the fact that many of these economies have failed to meet the condition of transition to competitive markets.

In order to more objectively assess the progress of these countries and their inclusion in global business flows, we will analyze some of the basic indicators of development.

Macroeconomics of Western Balkans in the Context of the Global Work and Business Environment, pp. 3–11
Copyright © 2022 by Information Age Publishing
www.infoagepub.com

ECONOMIC GROWTH

World Bank data predict gross domestic product (GDP) growth for the Western Balkans countries of 3.8% by 2022. Analyzed by countries of the region, the lowest GDP growth rate is projected for Northern Macedonia at 3.1%, and the highest for Serbia at 4% (Figure 1.1).

In Montenegro as a Mediterranean country, tourism has a great influence on GDP growth, that is, its share in GDP is almost 25% (Monstat, 2019), which speaks of its importance for the entire Montenegrin economy.

According to The Travel and Tourism Competitiveness 2019, Montenegro ranked 67th in 2019, while in 2017 it was ranked 72nd (World Economic Forum [WEF], 2019).

Guidelines for the development of Montenegrin tourism are defined in the document Montenegro Tourism Development Strategy to 2020 (2008), which was adopted for the period from 2008 to 2020. The defined strategic goals include the application of the principles and goals of sustainable development in order for Montenegro to expand and improve its position as a global top tourist destination. This should consequently result in the creation of new jobs for the citizens of Montenegro.

A slight increase in GDP is expected for Montenegro, that is, from 3% in 2019 to 3.2% in 2022. However, such a positive prognosis is subject to the influence of numerous risks, that is, it will depend on geopolitical and trade disputes to stagnation in the pace of structural reforms (World Bank, 2019).

These predictions were made before a new recession caused by the coronavirus could be foreseen. Therefore, economic growth rates will have to be adjusted. Some reports made after the crisis in mid-March 2020 expect a serious European recession of –4% in 2020, with a significant decline in production and employment (Pavlova, 2020).

EMPLOYMENT

In the countries of the European Union, a crawling growth of the employment rate was recorded in the observed period 2013–2019 (Figure 1.2), while all the countries of the Western Balkans recorded a higher growth than the EU countries with the highest employment (Figure 1.2).

Rates among the countries of the Western Balkans are in Albania and Serbia, while the most unfavorable situation is in Bosnia and Herzegovina. Namely, in the observed period, Serbia recorded the highest growth of the employment rate, that is, from 40.6 in 2013 to 49.7 in 2019 or an increase of 9.1 percentage points (World Bank, 2019a).

Observed employment trends for the last two years (2018–2020), it can be stated that employment growth continued in all countries of the region.

Figure 1.1

GDP Growth for tThe Countries of the Western Balkans With Projections Until 2022

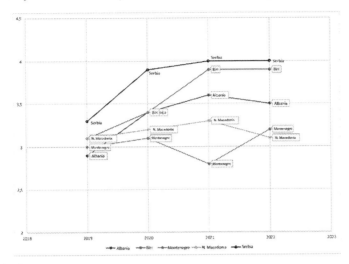

Source: Author.

Figure 1.2

Growth Rate Trend of Employment Rate in the Countries of the Western Balkans in Relation to the EU, 2013–2019

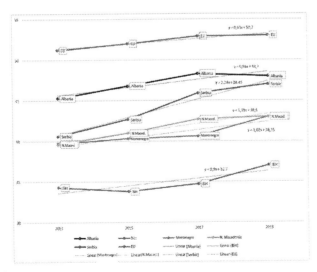

Source: Author.

This is confirmed by data that show that employment in June 2019 in the Western Balkans was higher by 2.4% compared to the same period last year. This created 149.430 new jobs in the labor market compared to the same period in 2018 (World Bank, 2019d).

The unemployment rate in Serbia dropped to 9.7% at the end of 2019 from 12.9% in the corresponding period of the previous year. The number of unemployed decreased by 24.6% and the number of employed increased by 4.3%. Meanwhile, the employment rate rose 2.3% from a year earlier (Trading Economics, 2020).

The WEF analysis (2019a) shows that the unemployment rate in Montenegro was 15.5% during 2019. According to Monstat (2019) data, out of the total number of active population or 289.5 thousand, 85.7% were employed and 14.3% unemployed.

The latest data from the Employment Agency of Montenegro (2020) show that 35.429 unemployed persons (20.516 women) were registered, which shows a slight increase of 111 persons or 0.31%. This was expected, given that the coronary virus pandemic had started in Montenegro and some employers had immediately started laying off workers.

The registered unemployment rate for December 2019 was 32.6% in Bosnia and Herzegovina, making this country the leader in the region Bosnia and Herzegovina Agency of Statistics (2019). Based on the data of the Agency of Statistics, the unemployment rate in Bosnia and Herzegovina in 2019 was 15.7% and was lower than in 2018 by 2.7 percentage points. On the other hand, the employment rate in 2019, amounted to 35.5% and is higher than the previous year by 1.2%.

New Models of Employment

In recent years, there has been an increase in new forms of employment. These include part-time, temporary, informal, and unpaid family work, especially among young women. Namely, thanks to the use of platforms in business and the emergence of the "gig economy," there are gradual changes in this domain. The selection of workers is not based on the employment of people who have certain knowledge, qualifications, and so forth, but a contract is concluded with the workers on the provision of a specific service (Radović-Marković & Tomaš 2019). In other words, over time, there is a gradual transition from stable or permanent employment to a "moonlighting" or "gig economy," which is characterized by temporary or contracted employment. This type of employment can be defined as "any job, but only of short or uncertain duration." In this way, an organization can fill in the gaps in skills and knowledge for certain jobs by temporarily hiring workers who possess those skills and knowledge.

According to statistical data, it can be stated that the share of the labor force in the EU-28, performing occasional jobs or working part-time, is constantly increasing, that is, from 14.9% in 2002 to 18.5% in 2018 (Eurostat, 2019). In addition, according to Eurostat (2019), 30.8% of employed women aged 20 to 64 worked part-time in EU countries compared to men, which was about 8.0% in 2018.

The World Bank report states that informal employment, one of the main challenges in the Western Balkans labor market, is still growing in Albania and Northern Macedonia, but is declining in Montenegro and Serbia. It is estimated that mostly young people, older women and less educated workers performed informal jobs in 2018 (World Bank, 2019a).

GENDER DIFFERENCES

In the female part of the population of the Western Balkans, there are reduced activity rates, lower incomes, high total unemployment, but also higher employment in less profitable sectors, with less representation compared to men in management positions, as well as among entrepreneurs (European Movement of Montenegro, 2013). Thus, in 2018, women's unemployment in the Western Balkans was 57% of the total number of unemployed (Global Markets, 2019). According to Global Markets (2019):

> Women are still struggling to achieve economic security. It is true that, compared to men, more women graduate from college, but only two out of five women in the Western Balkans have or are looking for work. It is estimated that every year the countries of the Western Balkans lose on average up to 18% of their GDP due to gender differences in the labor market. (Global Markets, 2019)

In Montenegro, there is insufficient protection of women in the labor market, especially those working in the informal economy (strongly expressed in tourism and hospitality), which results in increasing existential insecurity. The National Development Strategy of Montenegro 2008–2030 (2007) states that women in Montenegro can realize their potential and contribute to the overall sustainable development of society if they achieve equality as social actors. One of the key tasks of Montenegrin society is the economic and political empowerment of women and the adoption of gender-sensitive regulations and policies.

LABOR PRODUCTIVITY

The combination of GDP and employment data makes it possible to estimate labor productivity. According to the latest World Bank (2020) report, labor productivity has fallen in the Western Balkans by 5.4 percentage points. Since 2013 labor productivity growth in this region is almost zero. Consequently, the countries of the Western Balkans are less competitive on the international market compared to the EU countries, which have many times higher labor productivity.

According to the data of the World Bank (2019), in northern Macedonia, in the first half of 2019, real net wages increased by 2%, and in Serbia by 7.2% compared to the same period last year. Real wage growth was not in line with labor productivity.

The highest growth rates of minimum wages had Albania (18%), Montenegro (15%) and Serbia (11 %) (World Bank, 2019d).

PUBLIC AND FOREIGN DEBT

The public debt in Montenegro has increased significantly in the last 10 years or more. Namely, compared to 2008, when it amounted to only 29% of GDP, it doubled in the next five years, that is, according to the indicators of the Ministry of Finance of Montenegro, it reached 1.707 million euros, or 51.3% of GDP in October 2012 (Radović-Marković et al., 2013). However, at the end of 2012, the state debt of Montenegro decreased to 47.9% of GDP. According to the data of the Ministry of Finance, the public debt of Montenegro at the end of 2019 amounted to around 3.833 billion euros, which is 79.8% of the GDP. In addition to Montenegro's high public debt in 2019, it was 66.5% in Albania, while it was 52.4% in Serbia at the end of November (European Commission, 2020).

In response to the effects of the crisis, international financial institutions have recommended policies of fiscal consolidation and structural reforms in the Western Balkans. This has influenced the implementation of austerity measures in recent years in these countries to overcome the external and public debt, which have not been generally accepted among the inhabitants of these countries but have yielded results.

The greater capacity of EU countries to service their gross foreign debt creates a qualitative difference between their debt and the debt of the Western Balkan countries (Bartlett & Prica, 2017).

INVESTMENTS

The Western Balkans is struggling to attract foreign direct investment (FDI) and has therefore been working on reforms in recent years, with the ultimate goal of improving the business climate and fostering further integration in the regional and global markets (Jirasavetakul & Rahman,

2018; World Bank, 2019). Using its favorable geographical position, skilled workforce and lower wage costs than in Central Europe, the region had a large inflow of FDI in 2019.

According to the "World Investment Report 2019" of the UN Conference on Trade and Development (UNCTAD, 2019), Serbia had the largest inflow of foreign direct investment in the region with a growth of 44% ($4.1 billion), while Bosnia and Herzegovina had a growth of 4% ($ 468 million) and Albania of 13% ($1.3 billion). Northern Macedonia has tripled direct investment in the last two years, that is, from $205 million in 2017 to $737 million in 2019 (UNCTAD, 2019).

Montenegro is the only one in the region to record a 12% drop in direct investment. Namely, although Montenegro records the inflow of foreign investments, which in 2019 amounted to 712.8 million euros, at the same time 398 million euros flowed out of the country, which is 3.9% more than in the same period in 2018 (Central Bank of Montenegro, 2020). Further, in Montenegro, the structure of foreign investments has been changing in recent years, so that more has been invested in tourism, the banking sector and energy, while real estate investments are decreasing. The European Investment Bank (EIB) in the Western Balkans invests its funds in all countries in the region. Thus, it has provided EUR 40 million for Montenegro for the reconstruction of five main roads and thus improve the road network, which will contribute to tourism, trade, and regional integration. Tunnels and several bridges will be reconstructed, for which 1.5 million EUR of nonrefundable technical assistance has been allocated for Montenegro within the Economic Research Institute (ERI) program (EIB, 2019). It is also the first project in the Western Balkans to be supported by ERI by awarding grants.

Hungary's recently established "Western Balkans Green Centre" plans to make about 1.2 million euros available to launch green investments in Albania, Bosnia and Herzegovina, Kosovo, Montenegro, Northern Macedonia, and Serbia (Reporting Democracy, 2020). In this way, the "Green Centre" wants to help the region on the path to sustainable development, and at the same time to increase the international competitiveness of Hungarian companies that intend to invest in the green economy. In addition, they expect to be able to support the region's green transition and create new jobs.

In addition to these investments, the influence of China, Russia, and Turkey, which also want to continue investing in the Balkan region, has strengthened in recent years.

China has been strengthening its influence in this region since 2015, given that geographically, the Western Balkans is the final part of new China's silk sea route. In a short time, China has become the leading investor in some countries of the Western Balkans and is ranked as the number one foreign investor in Serbia (Krastev, 2018).

Chinese investors invest mainly in infrastructure, such as (Tomchev, 2017, p. 2):

- reconstruction of the Belgrade-Budapest railway;
- construction of the Bar-Boljare highway (which connects Montenegro and Serbia);
- construction of a highway between Albania and Montenegro;
- construction of highways in Albania, Bosnia and Northern Macedonia.

The Chinese need a presence in the Balkans in order to get closer to other European markets. In this regard, China is not facing resistance from small countries in the Balkans, given their investment needs and intention to reduce the gap for highly developed EU countries as soon as possible (the Western Balkans account for around 1% of EU GDP and are one of the most underdeveloped regions of Europe).

Turkey is also interested in investing in the Balkan region due to the need to connect economically and politically with countries with which it has cultural, religious, and other similarities. Thus, Turkish direct investments in Serbia, between 2015 and 2018, amounted to 133.7 million euros. Turkish companies took over 17 new projects in Serbia after 2018 with a value of 395.7 million dollars (New Economy, 2020). The projects refer, first of all, to the construction of the highway Belgrade—Sarajevo and Pojate—Preljina, where the Turkish company Enka will participate in a consortium with the American Bechtel.

By the end of June 2019, 2.162 companies were operating in Montenegro, formed by investors from Turkey (Bankar.me, 2019). Most of them are engaged in construction, consulting services, wholesale and retail trade, tourism and catering. Of the larger Turkish investments, those in the Nikšić Ironworks (Toščelik) and in the Port of Bar (Global ports) stand out. Turkey's Zirat Bank has opened a representative office in Montenegro, where it provides better banking services to Montenegrin and Turkish citizens living and working in Montenegro. In addition, LC Waikiki brand stores have been opened throughout the region.

Russia is also closely connected with the countries of the Western Balkans due to its historical and cultural relations. Especially in the energy sector, Russia has a significant influence, especially in Serbia, Bosnia, and Herzegovina and the North Macedonia, where crude oil and natural gas account for between 75 and 95% of imports from Russia (BOFIT, 2019 [No reference]). Therefore, the countries of the Western Balkans (except

Montenegro, which does not consume much gas) continue to support Russian infrastructure projects (e.g., Gazprom, South Stream, and TESLA) (Vladimirov et al., 2018).

CHAPTER 2

INCLUSION IN GLOBAL BUSINESS FLOWS

Mirjana Radović-Marković

COMPARISON OF THE GLOBALIZATION INDEX BETWEEN WESTERN BALKAN COUNTRIES

The Globalization Index (KOF) covers the economic, social, and political dimensions of globalization. The economic globalization that interests us here means the flow of money, capital, and transactions.

Among the countries of the Western Balkans, Montenegro had a globalization index of 72.05 in 2019, according to which it ranked 55th out of 203 ranked countries. Serbia was the best ranked country (36th place), and the worst positioned was Northern Macedonia (58th place). (Table 2.1).

Comparing the data for the last two years, it can be noticed that in all countries in the region there was an increase in the KOF index and that they improved their ranking except for Bosnia and Herzegovina, which recorded a decline (–7).

Montenegro advanced from 63rd place in 2017 to 55th place in 2019 (+8). Serbia also made progress in the period 2017–2019, that is (+10), Northern Macedonia advanced the most (+36), and Albania the least (+1).

Macroeconomics of Western Balkans in the Context of the Global Work and Business Environment, pp. 13–30
Copyright © 2022 by Information Age Publishing
www.infoagepub.com

Table 2.1

***KOF Globalization Index of the countries of the Western Balkans,
2017–2019***

Country	Globalization Index 2017	Rank	Globalization Index 2019	Rank
Serbia	69	46	78.98	36
N. Macedonia	55	94	70.79	58
Montenegro	65	63	72.05	55
Bosnia and Herzegovina	66.56	57	69.19	64
Albania	60	76	67.30	75

Source: KOF Index of Globalization, 2017 and 2019.

Among the countries in the region, Montenegro had the highest GDP
per capita and Albania the lowest.

The analysis of the impact of the globalization index on GDP growth per
capita showed dependence, that is, $R^2 = 0, 2082$ (Figure 2.1).

Figure 2.1

*Impact of Globalization (Measured by the Globalization Index) on GDP Per Capita for
the Countries of the Western Balkans*

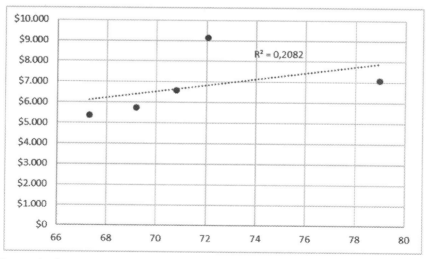

Source: Author.

Figure 2.1 shows that the effects of globalization on the economic growth of the countries of the Western Balkans depend on how much these economies are already integrated into the global economy. The less countries are involved in the global economy, the greater the positive impact of globalization and vice versa.

Namely, while the correlation between KOF and GDP for the countries of the Western Balkans is $R^2 = 0.2082$, this correlation is significantly lower for small countries that have a GDP per capita higher than U.S.\$25,000, that is, $R^2 = 0.0428$ (Radović-Marković & Tomaš, 2019).

THE IMPACT OF GLOBALIZATION ON COMPETITIVENESS

Globalization is influencing organizations around the world to be constantly on the lookout for achieving sustainable competitiveness. Measuring the competitiveness of national economies is of particular importance, as it contributes to business improvement and overall economic growth.

There are numerous interdependencies between globalization and competitiveness that the literature talks about. One approach focuses on the fact that in the last few decades, globalization has influenced the increasing integration of national and regional economies and the dominance of the world economy thanks to the expansion of multinational economies (Radović-Marković, 2011; Organisation for Economic Co-operation and Development [OECD], 2018).

Bang and Markeset (2011) emphasize that the main drivers of competitiveness growth under the influence of globalization are the following factors:

1. lower trade barriers.
2. lower transportation costs.
3. lower communication costs.
4. ICT development; and
5. dissemination of information technologies.

In line with global developments, digital transformation is particularly expected to play a vital role in fostering future sustainable growth in the Western Balkans region and contributing to regional cooperation.

Further, a number of scientists point out that the strategic choice of the company depends on enhancing the competitive advantages of the company in a global context. First of all, this primarily refers to the positioning of the company in the global market (Hitt & He, 2008).

Measuring the competitiveness of national economies is of particular importance, as it contributes to business improvement and overall economic growth. If the competitiveness on the global market is weak, then the national economy also suffers, which leads to protectionism, nontransparent state subsidies and barriers to market entry (Radović-Marković et al., 2013).

In terms of approaching the measurement of competitiveness at the organizational level, scientists emphasize that the resources of the firm have an impact on the behavior of the firm and its competitive advantages (Barney, 2007; Mahoney & Pandian, 1992). Although, according to them, all internal resources (physical, financial, human, and organizational resources) are of great importance for raising the competitiveness of the company, some of the scientists single out human and organizational resources as the most important in this regard (Zupan, 1996).

In the academic literature, a number of authors dealing with the competitiveness of organizations advocate for the growth of competitiveness through business processes. Consequently, firms must, through teamwork, increase their competence over time and thus contribute to their organization to increase competitiveness (King et al., 2001).

Scientists who put knowledge in the foreground believe that a firm can win a "competitive battle" only if it possesses more relevant knowledge than its competition (Inkpen, 1998; Zack, 1999). The allocation of intellectual capital as a key factor in the competitiveness of companies requires appropriate management. Accordingly, knowledge management is an activity that requires special competencies of strategic management of the company (Pucko, 1998). Companies operating in the global market base their competitive advantages on this theoretical approach (Radović-Marković et al., 2013).

Analysis of the survival of firms in the global market has shown that those who adopt innovations survive more often. In addition, the number of patents has been shown to be a reliable indicator of the existence of innovation. From this point of view, it was concluded that patents are closely related to a firm's productivity and its market value (Klette & Kortum, 2004). According to this conclusion, it can be expected that firms that use multiple patents will be more innovative and thus have an advantage over the competition (Helmers & Rogers, 2008).

Experiences of highly developed countries show that clusters are an effective instrument for strengthening the competitiveness of industrial enterprises, while clustering encourages the competitiveness of industry in the global market in three important ways—productivity growth, innovation, and the establishment of new enterprises (Mićić, 2010). In addition, it is interesting to note that many countries have increased their competitiveness thanks to a more efficient institutional environment, as confirmed by some research (Hitt & He, 2008).

Due to the changes brought about by globalization, the European Union has defined priority goals and instruments to ensure competitiveness, such as (Guide to the Europe 2020 Strategy, 2011):

1. strong support for knowledge development and innovation;
2. creating better conditions for investment;
3. stronger social cohesion.

The countries of the Western Balkans, which are in the phase of joining the European Union, have shown weaknesses in the field of administrative and innovation infrastructure, which brings them to the very back of Europe. These claims are argued by the competitiveness index of the countries in the region, which slows them down in terms of improving their market position. Therefore, it is necessary for them to go through different phases of legal, institutional, and real changes in the economic structure, the system of relations between economic entities, as well as in the behavioral manner (Radović-Marković et al., 2013).

In order for a country to enjoy sustainable economic growth and remain competitive internationally, the key lies in the government's investment in research and development and the launch of technological innovation. Namely, raising the competitiveness of the Western Balkan countries implies significant improvement of general competitiveness factors (macroeconomic stability and economic growth, involvement in global and integration processes, development of economic infrastructure, quality of science and technological development, quality of education and human potential, quality of management, etc.) (Radović-Marković et al., 2013).

Global Competitiveness Index

According to the latest methodology for determining the global competitiveness index, which was introduced in 2018, a detailed overview of factors and characteristics that stimulate productivity, economic growth and human development is provided.

The analysis of the global competitiveness index for 2019 shows that Montenegro, Serbia, Albania and Bosnia and Herzegovina are worse ranked compared to the previous year, that is (–2), (–7), (–5) and (–1), respectively. Unlike the mentioned countries, only Northern Macedonia has improved its rank (+2).

According to the WEF report (2019), based on the global competitiveness index, Montenegro ranks 73rd out of 141 economies, while Serbia ranked 76th according to the same report.

Putting in the ratio of GDP and the Global Competitiveness Index, a moderate dependence on $R^2 = 0.6028$ is observed (Figure 2.2).

Figure 2.2

Impact of GDP per capita on the Global Competitiveness Index

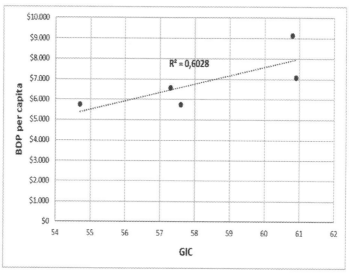

Source: World Economic Forum data (WEF, 2019).

THE IMPACT OF GLOBALIZATION ON INNOVATION

Schumpeter basically defined innovation as "a combination of developmental changes." Accordingly, taking into account the definitions of innovation in the literature, we can conclude that the general characteristics of innovation are the application of new ideas, the improvement of existing ones and inventions (Tekin & Tekdogan, 2015). They contribute and accelerate the development of new technology innovation processes (Kasper & Clohesi, 2008). In addition, fundamental changes are taking place globally as a result of the convergence of the innovation process and modern institutional changes. Namely, innovation becomes key to creating countries' strategic strengths (Held & McGrew, 2007, pp. 51–58).

The analysis of the connection between innovation and globalization in the conditions of modern trends in the economic development of Montenegro and other countries of the Western Balkans is at the centre of this part of the study. Accordingly, we will focus on the correlation between the KOF Globalization Index and the Global Innovation Index.

Global Innovation Index GII

The Global Innovation Index (GII) 2019 ranks innovation performance in 129 countries and economies around the world. The GII was jointly developed by Cornell University, the business school Insead based in Paris and VIPO. This global index includes more than 80 indicators that explore a wide range of innovations, including the political environment, education, infrastructure, and business sophistication (Table 2.2).

Table 2.2

Ranking of Western Balkan Countries According to GII, 2018–2019

	2018		2019	
Albania	83	30.3	83	30.3
Montenegro	52	36.5	45	37.7
Serbia	55	35.5	57	35.7
N. Maced.	84	29.9	59	35.3
BiH	77	31.1	76	31.4

Northern Macedonia made the most progress in ranking in 2019 compared to 2018, as its ranking increased by 25 positions, followed by Montenegro (+7) and Bosnia and Herzegovina (+1).

Albania remained in the same place in 2019 as in the previous year, while Serbia was the only country in the region to fall behind (−2).

The Innovation Capacity Index (ICI) serves to examine a wide range of policies and institutions that foster an innovation-friendly environment. This index is very complex and takes into account the following components: education, institutional environment, ICT application, scientific infrastructure and legal framework (Figure 2.3).

The innovation ecosystem consists of "innovation capacity" and "business dynamism."

According to the WEF report (2019), Montenegro was ranked 69th out of 141 economies in terms of " innovation capacity." In relation to Montenegro, Bosnia and Herzegovina was ranked worse according to the same report in terms of " innovation capacity," that is, it is at the bottom of this list with 117 place and is also the worst positioned of all five analyzed coun-

Figure 2.3

Innovation Capacity Index (ICI)

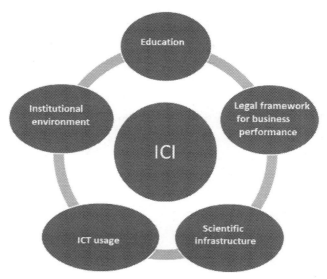

Source: Author.

tries in the region. Slightly better positioned than Bosnia and Herzegovina were Northern Macedonia with 97th place and Albania with 110th place. According to the same report, Serbia was the best ranked country in the Western Balkans with 59th position on the basis of "innovation capacity."

Various changes in the business environment have greatly affected the "business dynamism," that is, on the establishment and closure of companies, their productivity and competitiveness. Business dynamics statistics show that Montenegro was in 50th place according to WEF (2019) indicators, while Serbia was 54th immediately following Montenegro. According to the same report, Albania was ranked 63rd, followed by Northern Macedonia 65th and Bosnia and Herzegovina ranked 117th out of 141 countries.

It is necessary to emphasize the importance of a proper understanding of the importance of scientific infrastructure in the field of research on the growth of "innovation capacity," so that national policies in this area can be formed.

Innovation capacity in the Global Competitiveness Index is estimated on the basis of the following elements (Report of the National Science Council of the Republic of Serbia, 2018):

- Capabilities of existing economic entities to develop new designs or new top value-added products in order to be able to maintain competitiveness;
- Sufficient investment in research and development, especially by the private sector;
- Presence of high-quality scientific research institutions that can generate the basic knowledge needed to build new technologies;
- Extensive cooperation in research and technological development between universities and industry.

Figure 2.4

Quality of Scientific and Research Institutions in the Region

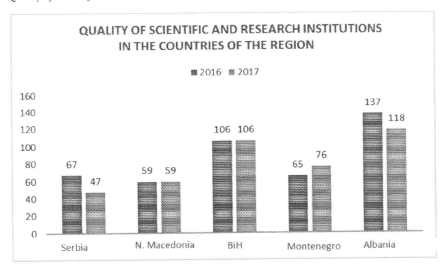

Source: Report of the National Council for Science of the Republic of Serbia (2018).

The data show that Montenegro is positioned high in terms of the quality of scientific and research institutions (65th place) and that it is the only one in 2017 in the region that has made progress compared to other countries in the region (Figure 2.4).

Comparing Montenegro with Romania, Croatia, Slovenia, and Bulgaria as members of the European Union from the environment, only the better position of Croatia (66th place) for 2017 can be noticed.

Infrastructure is among the first conditions for enriching knowledge and development of all sciences. By analyzing the scientific infrastructure in Serbia, it was determined that Serbian science is good because there are as many as 70 scientific institutes, but few of them are part of universities. Further, it is especially important to emphasize the high positioning of Serbian science among 148 countries in the world (see Table 2.3).

Table 2.3

Share of Western Balkan Countries in science in the Region of Eastern Europe and Number of Published Papers in the SCOPUS Database Cited, 1996–2018

Country	Rank	Documents	Cited documents	Number of citations	Citations by document	H-index[1]
Serbia	10	91,280	86,176	78,1607	8.56	220
Montenegro	23	3,920	21,019	21,019	5	51
BiH	19	12,226	11,504	70,210	5.74	91
N. Maced	20	11,949	11,312	21,019	9.18	108
Albania	22	4,727	4,445	30,255	6.4	62

Source: The author according to SJR data.

According to the SCOPUS,[1] database, the countries of the Western Balkans have increased the number of papers published in this reference database in the last two decades (Table 2.3). The comparison was made with the countries of Eastern Europe, consisting of 24 countries headed by the Russian Federation.

Despite the gradual growth of the number of papers and their citations, the countries of the Western Balkans are ranked the worst, except for Serbia, which in the analyzed period was above the middle of the list of countries (Position 10).

Data for Montenegro (23rd place), as well as Albania (22nd place), Northern Macedonia (20th place) and Bosnia and Herzegovina (19th place), support the claims that scientists from the mentioned countries were not interested enough in publishing in journals on SCOPUS. The reasons can be numerous, that is, from insufficient familiarity with journals from this database to insufficient evaluation of these journals by national ministries of science. It is necessary to emphasize that Serbia is continuously increasing its share in the region of Eastern Europe, as well as the number of published papers cited in SCOPUS. This was especially contributed by the adoption of the Rulebook on the procedure, evaluation, and quantitative presentation of scientific research results of researchers, where scientific papers published in journals indexed in SCOPUS are valued (Official Gazette of the Republic of Serbia, 2016).

Observed in the last few years (Figure 2.5), scientists from Bosnia and Herzegovina have mostly increased the number of published papers in journals included in the SCOPUS database, that is, by 412 papers. On the other hand, Northern Macedonia was the only one in the region to have a decrease in the number of published papers in 2018 compared to 2015 (SJR, 2019).

Figure 2.5

Number of Papers Published in the Countries of the Western Balkans in 2015 and 2018

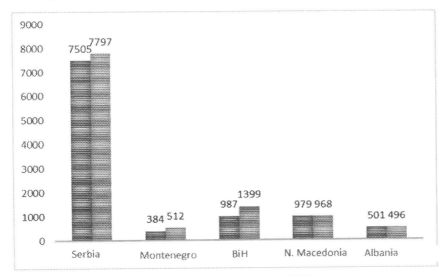

Source: The author according to SJR data (2015 and 2018).

Given the fact that the SCOPUS index database includes 60% more journals than the WoS database, it is natural to expect that the number of papers by researchers will be higher in the SCOPUS database (National Council for Scientific and Technological Development of the Republic of Serbia, 2018).

According to the available data in the last three years, researchers at DHN from Serbia have published only 43 prominent monographs of international importance (M11) out of a total of 6.200 published books.

In addition, in February 2018, out of 125 registered innovative organizations, only two worked in the field of social innovation, but none was accredited to conduct research.

Obviously, there is a huge potential for improvement in this domain, because technological innovations always require social innovations. Unfortunately, this potential was not used at all by researchers at DHN.

The mobility of researchers is limited, while the presence of foreign scientists in DHN research and higher education institutions is almost nonexistent.

In Montenegro, like Serbia, the Ministry of Science is a great advocate of opening national science to EU countries and other countries. Thus, in the middle of 2019, a document was adopted that refers to the issues of open access to the research infrastructure. In this way, interdisciplinarity, international and intersectoral mobility are encouraged and numerous opportunities for cooperation are created. Namely, open access avoids duplication of equipment and saves funds for other investments in science. The results published by the Ministry of Science of Montenegro (2019) showed the good condition of existing equipment, whose total value is estimated at 28 million euros, of which 67% has been invested in the last six years. These data testify to a significant increase in investment in scientific infrastructure.

Further, in 2019, the Ministry of Science of Montenegro initiated the procedure of registration in the Register of Innovative Organizations in accordance with the Law on Innovative Activity (Official Gazette of Montenegro, 2018). According to the available data in Montenegro, 33 innovative organizations are registered in the Register, as follows: 13 scientific research institutions, 18 business entities, 1 innovation and entrepreneurship center and 1 center of excellence (Ministry of Science of Montenegro, 2019).

In addition to Montenegro and Serbia, other countries in the region have made significant efforts in recent years to develop the scientific structure and encourage innovation. They have adopted various strategies, laws, and programs to improve the performance of the sector at the national level and have improved regional R&D cooperation, for example by committing to the "Regional Strategy for Innovation and Innovation Development of the Western Balkans" (SEE, 2020) (see Figure 2.6).

Figure 2.7 shows that the calculated correlation coefficient R^2 is 0.4048 and this value indicates a moderately high degree of positive linear correlation between the KOF Globalization Index and the Global Innovation Index for the countries of the Western Balkans. Research on the relationship between innovation and the globalization index also shows that countries that are highly involved in the globalization process have a higher rank in terms of innovation. In other words, the more globally integrated countries are, the more favorable conditions are for the development of an innovative economy. Accordingly, many countries are making great efforts to increase the innovation of their economies and thus ensure greater competitiveness in the global market. Namely, the

Figure 2.6

Global Innovation Index 2018–2019

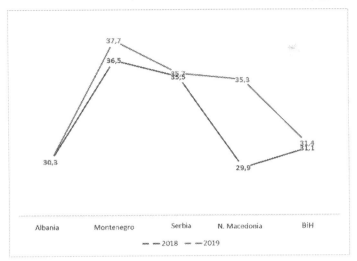

Source: The authors according to http://statisticstimes.com/ranking/global-innovation-index.php

Figure 2.7

Correlation Between KOF Index and GII

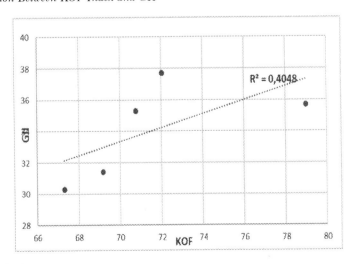

Source: Author.

state can play a major role in innovation, as well as in the development of an environment that supports research and development. Through its measures, it can encourage the mobility of researchers through facilitating international cooperation, as well as through financial support for research. In Serbia, Montenegro and other Western Balkan countries, the structure of international scientific cooperation is mainly dominated by projects, which are being done with some European countries. Montenegro, Serbia, Bosnia and Herzegovina and Northern Macedonia have joined the Horizon 2020 platform, the largest program for research and innovation of the European Union, which envisages the arrival of key scientific discoveries, inventions and innovations, and their market application.

To the extent that start-ups play a role in innovation and job creation, the region should be concerned. Therefore, many countries in the region have started taking measures to encourage start-ups. For example, the Ministry of Science of Montenegro has launched a program to encourage innovative start-ups (2019–2021). This program should contribute to the creation of attractive conditions for the Montenegrin innovative ecosystem, with a focus on innovative start-ups (ZUNS, 2019).

The Impact of GDP Per Capita on Innovation Growth

In the analysis, we also compared the level of GDP per capita with the current values in the Western Balkan countries from 2019 with their levels of innovation (Figure 2.8).

It is not surprising that it can be seen from the graph that the innovation capacity and GDP per capita are in a moderate correlation $R^2 = 0.6212$.

Despite the fact that there is a high correlation between GDP and innovation levels, the low level of allocations for science and technological development in the region (0.3–0.4% of GDP), which is significantly lower than the European average and 2% of GDP, does not provide an opportunity for further significant development of science in perspective. For these reasons, there is an increasing insistence that the lack of funding for research be compensated through international cooperation, where research costs are passed on to project partner countries.

Given that the development of science in each country relies on the efforts of its own nation, it is at the same time influenced by international scientific cooperation. "With this in mind, it can be concluded that international scientific cooperation is an important component of a society's orientation towards the development of scientific achievements" (Radović-Marković, 2019a). It is important for such projects that they provide equipment, exchange of knowledge and experience and scholarships for the most talented young researchers.

Figure 2.8

The Impact of GDP Per Capita on GII

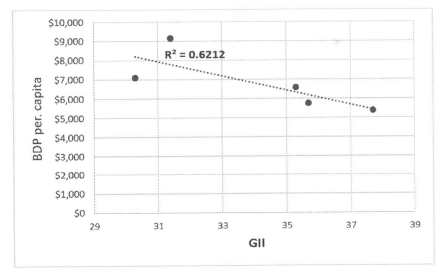

Source: Author.

Regional governments will face a huge range of challenges over the next five years, from addressing bilateral issues, unemployment, and public debt, to aligning demands with Union policies and resolving the current brain drain crisis by strengthening international scientific and economic cooperation with EU and U.S. member states where most diasporas from the region live. Strengthening economic and scientific ties with the diaspora would reduce the brain drain from the region (Radović-Marković, 2019a).

With the support of the World Bank, innovation funds have been created in Northern Macedonia and Serbia, and one will soon be created in Montenegro as well. They have funded successful programs, but they are still "too fragmented to attract additional investment, especially outside the region" (WEF, 2020).

The Impact of Education on Innovation

Education is one of the most important factors for forecasting the future economic and development results of a country. It is a prerequisite for economic competitiveness and one of the necessary attributes of a functioning market.

The countries of the Western Balkans in this domain constantly have a worse result than the EU members, which leads to the conclusion that the quality of education systems in the region is low (EBRD, 2016). Further, the connection between the economy and educational institutions is insufficient. In addition, functional illiteracy remains a problem in almost all Western Balkan countries, with Albania of a functional illiteracy rate of 60%.

The relative importance of technology and innovation adoption to improve productivity has increased in recent years, as progress in expanding the relationship of knowledge and the increasing use of information and communication technologies (ICT) (López-Claros & Mata, 2009).

The European Union has encouraged its strategic intentions to build an information society under strategies related to: the EU digital agenda, innovative Europe, new skills and jobs, putting young people at the forefront of development by 2025, as well as the development of ICT in new industrial policy. Investments in ICT contribute to the general improvement of the functioning of enterprises (OECD, 2010) through the process of internal and external cooperation on innovations, which are slower than the technological advances themselves.

New forms of work, new technologies and new demands placed on employees, have gradually led to a redefinition of education and to directing individuals and educational institutions in that direction. Training of human resources for certain jobs is performed primarily in terms of increasing the knowledge and competencies of employees, with the intention to better respond to work tasks (Radović-Marković, 2011a, p. 39). In recent years, general competencies have been specifically considered in education research (Barth et al., 2007; Canto-Sperber, Dupuy, 2001; Holmes & Hooper, 2000).

Researchers Allen and Van der Velden (2005) developed a methodology according to which highly educated personnel are expected to develop at least five areas of general competence:

1. Professional expertise: highly educated people are expected to become experts in their professional field;
2. Functional flexibility: implies that highly educated personnel must be able to respond to new challenges and quickly acquire new knowledge;
3. Innovation and knowledge management: highly educated people are expected to, in addition to successfully performing work tasks, create an environment in which to manage knowledge-based innovation;
4. Mobilization of human resources: highly educated personnel are expected to be able to mobilize all available human resources and direct them in the desired direction;

5. International orientation: given the processes of globalization, highly educated people are expected to be strongly internationally oriented.

Some authors necessarily include experience in the integral part of competencies in addition to education (Bassellier et al., 2003; Rockart et al., 1996). Experience in the application of information technology refers to the activities undertaken in the company in the field of information technology projects and experience in managing these projects.

According to some research, the competencies of managers will influence the development of the organization and the training of employees (Tippins & Sohi, 2003).

Product and process innovation is often determined by the market in which the firm operates but is closely linked to the role of managers and their impact on the company's innovative strategy.

Managerial IT competencies must include the following areas of IT competencies: technology, engineering and management, intellectuality, and learning (Figure 2.9).

Managers, creative leaders, can use a wide range of new, technologically supported options in formulating their strategies. They are increasingly using it in business to meet changes, not just react to them. Therefore, it is necessary to permanently increase the skills of managers and the environment for continuous improvement through learning, in order to use IT tools to expand innovative skills in business (Barrios et al., 2003; Bessant et al., 2001).

Modern research also shows that workforce agility can be achieved through "cross-training of workers," since cross-trained workers are much more flexible than other workers (Foss & Knudsen, 2000). Accordingly, universities will need to expand and revise their curricula if they are to educate students for a digital future that is inclusive, sustainable, and collaborative. Namely, greater progress is needed in the preparation of the countries of the Western Balkans for the fourth industrial revolution, that is innovation power in business; this would reduce the gap with Western Europe. The special need to strengthen technical and vocational education should be emphasized in order to facilitate the interaction between educational institutions and the business community and to enable graduates with specialized skills to more easily adapt to the needs of the economy. So, in addition to preparing us for work, education should also encourage creativity and innovative skills, where the deep influences of philosophy, ethics, organizational behavior, politics, and art intertwine in addition to computer knowledge.

Figure 2.9

Model of Managerial IT Competencies

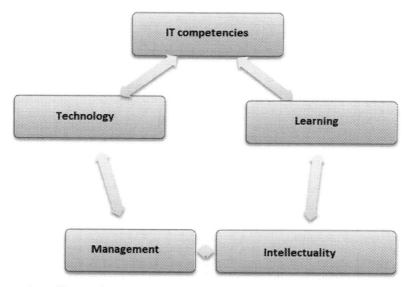

Source: Bassellier et al. (2003).

CONCLUSION

Western Balkan countries should without any doubt continue in the perspective of internal reforms. In addition, having in mind that they are all small countries, the only way for it to achieve economic growth and become economically more relevant in the global framework is for them to in greater extent than before internationalize their business activities. That implies that they should become a more serious "global player." However, the manner in which the positioning of small and medium enterprises will be done in the global market will depend on their potentials and limitations-resources available, as well as their ability to react to variable change on the market.

NOTE

1. The SCOPUS index database (published by Elsevier) currently includes 22.794 scientific journals from the natural, technical, medical, and social sciences, of which 3.643 are fully open access.

CHAPTER 3

REMOTE WORK IN THE WESTERN BALKANS COUNTRIES

Mirjana Radović-Marković

INTRODUCTION

Work from home, teleworking, remote office—it has several names, but no matter what you call it, it means working in an environment that is not the company's office. The work is mostly done, but not necessarily in the house of the worker. However, workers may choose another place to conduct business activities, such as a warehouse, workshop, or other space, provided that it is not the employer's space.

Due to COVID-19, work from home has actualized, which otherwise has a very long tradition. Not all organizations and their employees had equal conditions to work in this way due to their occupation, home conditions or other factors. What applies to individuals also applies to regions and nations: Thus, some countries have shown greater flexibility and the power to adapt than other. The research team from MIT recently created an index that analyzes the economic impact of remote work in 30 countries (Bana et al., 2020). The results of these studies have shown that developed economies are likely to fare better—especially those countries with greater diversification of industries and occupations that are more conducive to

Macroeconomics of Western Balkans in the Context of the Global Work and Business Environment, pp. 31–59
Copyright © 2022 by Information Age Publishing
www.infoagepub.com

working from home, along with support conditions such as internet access. Regions where it is harder to work from home may be more vulnerable to layoffs and reduced economic activities.

Whether working from home is the product of one's own choice or is the result of a pandemic or other environmental shock, the change in the way work is done is real and governments must understand the implications and take steps to position their economies accordingly.

Grant et al. (2019) among the many factors that are important for remote work, highlight the trust of colleagues and managers. On the other hand, Baruch (2000) believes that self-discipline, the ability to work independently, self-organization, self-confidence, time management skills and computer literacy are of particular importance for remote work.

FREELANCERS VERSUS SELF-EMPLOYED

In the past, individuals believed in the importance of maintaining a long career as an employee of a company and therefore never applied for freelance jobs. Freelance work, which was well paid, was also not available to professionals who wanted to leave the corporate world. However, times are changing, which has been reflected in a large increase in the number of freelancers in the world.

In previous research, the entrepreneurial role of freelancers has been neglected, given that mostly the research conducted on freelancers was motivated by other areas of the labor market, and not by the essential interest in these self-employed workers. In the entrepreneurial literature, freelancers are often categorized as a version of an entrepreneur or manager (Burke, 2011).

Very often one can come across an opinion that puts a sign of equality between the self-employed and freelancers. However, there are significant differences between the two terms. First of all, self-employment has a much broader meaning than being a freelancer. In a sense, the essential meaning of self-employment is not "traditional employment."

A self-employed person can do business with other employees or use freelancers (Radović-Marković & Tomaš, 2019). Thus, while freelancers are self-employed, a self-employed person may not be a freelancer (Pascoe, 2019). This is where the confusion arises. To solve it, it is enough to say that a freelancer is just a type of self-employed worker.

Unlike people who are self-employed and often run their own business and can employ other people, a freelancer is a self-employed person who has no employees. In other words, a freelancer means one person who works independently and does different projects for different companies. He mainly works on a number of short-term contracts.

Freelancing has enjoyed impressive growth in recent years in all considered countries.

There are several reasons for freelancer expansion (Radović-Marković et al., 2021):

- It is a way to generate additional income for debt repayment or savings.
- It is easy to start if the individual already has the necessary skills and equipment to do the job.
- It enables greater independence in relation to permanent employment in a company.
- It is often flexible and allows you to work part-time or outside the working hours.

The freelancer can choose the clients he will work for. But once he does, he loses control of the project he will work on and has no impact on the deadline for completion of the work. In contrast to freelancers, the self-employed enjoy a high level of control, because no one puts pressure on them. They can plan the deadlines for the completion of the work themselves.

In many countries, freelancers may choose to pay or not pay taxes. Their sole responsibility is to comply with the country's tax rules. No one will follow them specifically because of taxes, because they would mostly work from home. It is therefore up to the freelancer to check with the tax regulator for any of the different types of taxes he must meet. On the other hand, people who call themselves self-employed must pay local and state taxes provided by law. The self-employed will even have to spend part of the income on the payment of employees' salaries in case they have them.

TECHNOLOGICAL INFRASTRUCTURE

The internet infrastructure gives a significant advantage to many countries having decided to work from home. The results of research by experts from MIT show that no country in the world is fully ready for all its inhabitants to work from home (Bana et al., 2020). Consequently, regions that specialize in industries dealing with occupations that require immediate physical proximity are more vulnerable than other regions with more balanced economies.

According to the data of Global 2020 (Figure 3.1), Northern Macedonia is the best ranked country among those analyzed, that is, it has the highest internet penetration rate compared to Serbia, Montenegro, and Bosnia and Herzegovina. Although Bosnia and Herzegovina are ranked the worst among these countries, the number of internet users in Bosnia and Herzegovina recorded the highest growth between 2019 and 2020 (+10%).

Figure 3.1

Internet Penetration in %

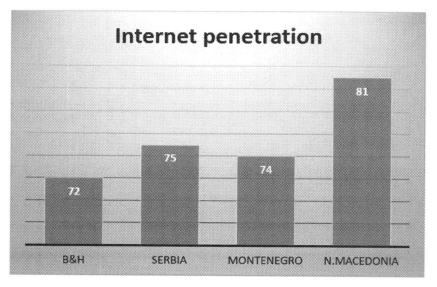

Source: Author preparing according to Digital 2020.

Despite the fact that Northern Macedonia has as much as 81% internet penetration, it has only 13% of the employed population working from home according to the 2020 Skills Toward Employability and Productivity Survey (Ross, 2020). On the other hand, about 15% of the employed population worked from home in Serbia during 2020 despite having 75% internet penetration in the country (BIZLife, 2020). The reason for this is that Northern Macedonia did not make sufficient use of digitalization opportunities, as well as the lack of digital skills of workers. Education, digital skills, and gender are very closely linked. Therefore, it is necessary for digitalization policy to address all these aspects simultaneously.

In order for the countries of the Western Balkans to maximize the impact of the internet and new technologies, significant investments in infrastructure are needed. The significance of digitalization has been recognized in the Republic of Serbia, resulting in reforms, economic growth, education, and digitalization being among the main priorities of the Government. So, Serbia has improved its score in 4G investment over the last year (Digital Serbia, 2020). It is expected that investments will be made in 5G infrastructure by 2025. The combination of the 5G network, the use of IoT data and artificial intelligence will transform the labor market.

The Digital Agenda for the Western Balkans (European Commission, 2018) aims to support the region's transition to a digital economy. One of the most tangible results of digital integration for the citizens of the Western Balkans is the zero roaming fee agreement that began several years ago and will be completed till July 2021.

At the company level, there is also great heterogeneity in how much organizations support employees in working from home. As the pandemic continues, so is the growing focus on the use of digital technologies. Thanks to the Internet and modern technologies, some organizations have built an excellent foundation for working from home, while others have not. Some have software that helps employees organize tasks more easily and quickly, and plan their responsibilities and working hours. This contributes to simple and efficient remote operation. In addition, the pandemic has fuelled innovation in digital tools and platforms and increased the digitalization of business processes. However, in order for digital tools and software to meet their purpose, training in the use of technologies is necessary. As a result of this development, the need for a digitally competent workforce has increased.

Digital skills are becoming an important prerequisite for employment worldwide. Those with the lowest levels of digital skills would be most affected, as well as those who are least willing to upgrade their skills (Vučeković et al., 2020). Competencies can be gained through education, and training. Given the importance of digital skills, the European Commission has set targets in the European Skills Agenda and the Digital Education Action Plan to ensure that 70% of adults have basic digital skills by 2025 (European Commission, 2021). The Digital Education Action Plan (2021–2027) sets out the European Commission's vision for high-quality, inclusive digital education in Europe (European Commission, 2021a). The experiences gained by the countries of the European Union, as well as the countries of the Western Balkans from the COVID-19 crisis, during which they used new technologies in education, should in the future make education systems even more adapted to the digital age.

RESEARCH GOALS

In order to assess the potential gain for the economies of the selected countries of the Western Balkans by adopting a more flexible work culture, the current attitudes of the population of Serbia, Montenegro, Northern Macedonia and Bosnia and Herzegovina were examined. This research aimed to create a picture of the extent to which this way of working has been adopted in the mentioned countries, the work motives of those entrepreneurs who run their business from home, potential obstacles, and limitations of employees in this way.

In addition, the aim of our research is to examine how the pandemic has affected the operations of organizations in Serbia and the scope of their operations, as well as how it has affected employees who work from home and remotely. Moreover, we explore both subjective and objective dimensions of job quality, such as job satisfaction, motivation, along with issues related work-life balance.

The study also identifies the extent to which the ability to work remotely could enable workers to use their working time more efficiently and encourage nonemployed people to reenter the labor market.

Understanding how the combination of occupations, technological infrastructure and demographic characteristics in the region has affected the ability of people to work from home can help policy makers and organization owners, as well as future entrepreneurs, prepare for this mode of work.

METHODOLOGY

The study was conducted in four countries. Further, the research is based on a review of the existing literature and our previous research. Of the qualitative methods, a web survey[1] was used, which contains a structured questionnaire of 22 questions. Before sending the survey, the respondents were explained the importance of the research and its context. In addition, a comparative method was used, which served to compare the results of the research obtained in this way and put them in relation to the collected data for four countries—Serbia, Bosnia and Herzegovina, Montenegro, and Northern Macedonia. Another method of analysis and synthesis has found its application in this study. Of the quantitative methods, the Chi-Square test and the Mann-Whitney test were used.

At the end of June 2020, the research began. Data were collected by October of the same year on a total sample of 1.031 respondents. The size of the sample by countries taken into consideration was 408 respondents for Serbia, 201 respondents for Montenegro and Bosnia and Herzegovina and 221 respondents for Northern Macedonia.

Upon completion of the survey, the collected data were coded, tabulated, and analyzed in accordance with the conceptual framework and objectives of the study. Descriptive techniques were used to analyze the collected data using appropriate software, such as SPSS and Microsoft Excel.

Descriptive analyses, such as range, number, percentage, mean, standard deviation, and ranking order, were used whenever possible.

Three broad groups are targeted: currently individuals who work from home as freelancers, entrepreneurs who are self-employed, as well as those individuals who work remotely for the needs of the companies where they are employed. The methodology contains method design for data collection and data analysis.

RESEARCH RESULTS AND DISCUSSIONS

When asked what should be followed when working from home, we received very different answers for the analyzed countries (Figure 3.2).

First of all, the respondents from Montenegro were mostly guided by cost savings around renting office space when choosing to run a home-based business (32.8%), while this factor was the least important for the respondents from Serbia (22.1%).

For the respondents from Bosnia and Herzegovina, the most important thing to decide to do business from home is the opportunity to balance professional with private and family obligations (39.3%), and then for the respondents from Serbia (29.4%). This factor was of approximate importance for the other two analyzed countries, Montenegro and Bosnia and Herzegovina, that is, about 21%.

A good business idea was almost equally important for the respondents from Bosnia and Herzegovina (25.4%) and Northern Macedonia (24.4%), while it was the least important for the respondents from Montenegro (18.9%).

It is interesting that for all countries, earning additional income was of the least importance, among other determining factors, to work from home. Thus, only 7.5% of respondents from Montenegro thought that this factor was important for them.

Significant differences can also be confirmed by applying Chi-Square Tests (Table 3.1).

Eight cells (28.6%) have expected count less than 5. The minimum expected count is 39.

In contrast to motivational factors where greater differences were observed among the analyzed countries, slightly smaller differences were observed when it comes to the basic rules for successful business from home (Figure 3.3).

For the respondents from Serbia and Northern Macedonia, good technical and technological equipment (24.4%) is of equal importance for successful business from home. Communication skills are also equally important in these two countries (23.6%). For the respondents from

Figure 3.2

Entrepreneur's Motives for Working From Home

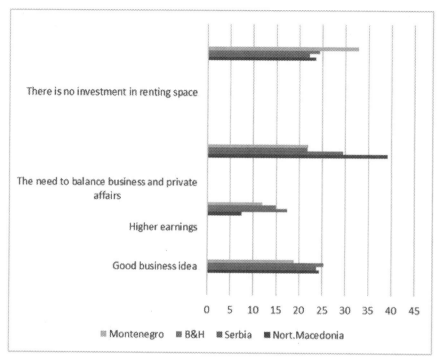

Source: The Author.

Table 3.1

Chi-Square Tests

	Value	*df*	Asymp. Sig. (2-sided)
Pearson Chi-Square	65.689[a]	18	.000
Likelihood Ratio	68.141	18	.000
Linear-by-Linear Association	1.461	1	.227
N of Valid Cases	1,031		

Source: Author.

Figure 3.3

Basic Rules for Successful Doing Business From Home

Source: Author.

Bosnia and Herzegovina, work experience was the least important (8.7%), while for Northern Macedonia it was of the greatest importance (20.9%) compared to respondents from other analyzed countries, who stated the importance of experience for doing business from home. Small differences have emerged between countries in terms of the importance of workspaces.

For the purposes of this research, one of the questions we asked the respondents referred to the fact how much family members participate in doing business from home (Table 3.2).

Comparing the obtained results, significant differences were noticed, which were confirmed by Chi-Square Tests (Table 3.3).

Thus, in Bosnia and Herzegovina and Serbia, only 10% and 11% respectively, family members work and participate in the business. The reason for this is the fact, that they did not show interest in getting involved. For the other two countries analyzed this percentage is twice as high (Table 3.2).

One of the questions addressed to the respondents from the analyzed four countries, referred to degree of engagement in jobs from home. For our study, it is of special importance whether it is about permanent or additional work (Table 3.4).

Table 3.2

Have You Included Other Members of Your Family in Your Regular Business Activities at Home?

			Country				
			Bosnia and Her-zegovina	Monte-negro	Northern Macedonia	Serbia	Total
Have you included other members of your family in your regular business activities at home? In case none of the offered answers corresponds, enter the answer in the section "Other"	They only have an advisory role and support me	Count	60	58	45	93	256
		% within What country do you live in?	29.9%	28.9%	20.4%	22.8%	24.8%
	I have because they also participate in my business from home	Count	20	43	46	45	154
		% within What country do you live in?	10.0%	21.4%	20.8%	11.0%	14.9%
	I haven't, since they don't have a contract with the employer	Count	36	44	48	76	204
		% within What country do you live in?	17.9%	21.9%	21.7%	18.6%	19.8%
	I have not considering that they do not have the qualifications to perform those jobs.	Count	1	0	0	0	1
		% within What country do you live in?	.5%	0.0%	0.0%	0.0%	.1%
	I have not, other reasons	Count	11	4	4	30	49
		% within What country do you live in?	5.5%	2.0%	1.8%	7.4%	4.8%
	No, since they are not interested in getting involved	Count	73	52	78	164	367
		% within What country do you live in?	36.3%	25.9%	35.3%	40.2%	35.6%
Total		Count	201	201	221	408	1,031
% within What country do you live in?			100.0%	100.0%	100.0%	100.0%	100.0%

Source: Author.

Table 3.3

Chi-Square Tests

	Value	df	Asymp. Sig. (2-sided)
Pearson Chi-Square	50.758[a]	15	.000
Likelihood Ratio	51.262	15	.000
Linear-by-Linear Association	7.925	1	.005
N of Valid Cases	1,031		

a. 4 cells (16.7%) have expected count less than 5. The minimum expected count is .19.

Source: Author.

Table 3.4

Is the Engagement Needed for Full-Time or Part-Time Work?

			What country do you live in?				
			Bosnia and Herzegovina	Montenegro	Northern Macedonia	Serbia	Total
Is the engagement needed for full-time or part-time?	I do not know	Count	1	5	4	5	15
		% within What country do you live in?	.5%	2.5%	1.8%	1.2%	1.5%
	This is a job without working hours	Count	45	59	74	152	330
		% within What country do you live in?	22.4%	29.4%	33.5%	37.3%	32.0%
	The additional working hours	Count	12	19	42	26	99

(Table continued on next page)

Table 3.4 (Continued)

Is the Engagement Needed for Full-Time or Part-Time Work?

		What country do you live in?				
		Bosnia and Herzegovina	Montenegro	Northern Macedonia	Serbia	Total
Full time	% within What country do you live in?	6.0%	9.5%	19.0%	6.4%	9.6%
	Count	43	57	65	126	291
It depends on whether we have another job	% within What country do you live in?	21.4%	28.4%	29.4%	30.9%	28.2%
	Count	100	61	36	99	296
	% within What country do you live in?	49.8%	30.3%	16.3%	24.3%	28.7%
Total	Count	201	201	221	408	1,031
% within What country do you live in?		100.0%	100.0%	100.0%	100.0%	100.0%

Source: Author.

The comparative analysis of the results for the selected countries showed significant differences confirmed by Chi-Square Tests (Table 3.5).

Based on the obtained data, it can be concluded that mostly the respondents in the North Macedonia opted for part-time work from home (19%), while the percentage in other countries ranges between 6 and 9.5%. Mostly employed full-time are in Serbia (30.9%), and the least in Bosnia and Herzegovina (21.4%). It should be especially emphasized that in all countries, an average of 32% of respondents share the same opinion that working from home is without working hours, that is, that they are constantly devoted to it.

The answers to the question "What strategies do you use to increase earnings?", also showed significant differences among respondents' opinions in all four countries (Table 3.6).

Table 3.5

Chi-Square Tests

	Value	df	Asymp. Sig. (2-sided)
Pearson Chi-Square	90.860[a]	12	.000
Likelihood Ratio	85.054	12	.000
Linear-by-Linear Association	27.194	1	.000
N of Valid Cases	1,031		

a. 3 cells (15,0%) have expected count less than 5. The minimum expected count is 2.92.

Source: Author.

The analysis showed that the majority of respondents do not have a specific strategy in Montenegro (35.8%), while in other countries the percentage ranged between 24 and 28.7%. The highest percentage of those who rely on the advice of other experts was in Northern Macedonia (29.4%), while the percentage was lowest in Bosnia and Herzegovina (5.5%).

According to Table 3.6. it can be seen that the respondents from Bosnia and Herzegovina.

Table 3.6

What Strategies Do You Use to Increase Earnings?

			What country do you live in?				
			Bosnia and Herzegovina	Montenegro	Northern Macedonia	Serbia	Total
What strategies do you use to increase earnings? In case none of the offered answers	Other I go to professional seminars and get professional certificates	Count	5	0	0	6	11
		% within What country do you live in?	2.5%	0.0%	0.0%	1.5%	1.1%
		Count	13	16	19	38	86

(Table continued on next page)

Table 3.6 (Continued)

What Strategies Do You Use to Increase Earnings?

		What country do you live in?				
		Bosnia and Herzegovina	Montenegro	Northern Macedonia	Serbia	Total
I go to professional seminars and get professional certificates	Count	13	16	19	38	86
	% within What country do you live in?	6.5%	8.0%	8.6%	9.3%	8.3%
I have no specific strategy	Count	53	72	53	117	295
	% within What country do you live in?	26.4%	35.8%	24.0%	28.7%	28.6%
I rely on expert advice	Count	11	19	65	48	143
	% within What country do you live in?	5.5%	9.5%	29.4%	11.8%	13.9%
I exchange experiences with other colleagues from the same industry	Count	67	56	44	137	304
	% within What country do you live in?	33.3%	27.9%	19.9%	33.6%	29.5%
I constantly follow the professional literature and get additional education	Count	52	38	40	62	192
	% within What country do you live in?	25.9%	18.9%	18.1%	15.2%	18.6%
Total	Count	201	201	221	408	1,031
% within What country do you live in?		100.0%	100.0%	100.0%	100.0%	100.0%	

Source: Author.

The big difference between countries in terms of strategies you use to increase earnings was confirmed by Chi-Square Tests (Table 3.7).

Table 3.7

Chi-Square Tests

	Value	df	Asymp. Sig. (2-sided)
Pearson Chi-Square	87.451[a]	15	.000
Likelihood Ratio	85.085	15	.000
Linear-by-Linear Association	3.921	1	.048
N of Valid Cases	1,031		

a. 4 cells (16.7%) have expected count less than 5. The minimum expected count is 2.14.

Further, the analysis showed that most employees worked from home for a long time between 0 and 5 years. This number is particularly pronounced in Bosnia and Herzegovina (89.6%) and Montenegro (76.6%) (Table 3.8).

Table 3.8

How Long Have You Been Working From Home?

			Country				
			Bosnia amd Herzegovina	Monte-negro	North-ern Mace-donia	Serbia	Total
How long have you been working from home	0 to 5 years	Count	180	154	140	284	758
	% within What country do you live in?						

(Table continued on next page)

Table 3.8 (Continued)

How Long Have You Been Working From Home?

		Country				
		Bosnia amd Herze-govina	Monte-negro	North-ern Mace-donia	Serbia	Total
		89.6%	76.6%	63.3%	69.6%	73.5%
	6 to 10 years	17	30	56	79	182
How long have you been working from home		8.5%	14.9%	25.3%	19.4%	17.7%
	11 to 15 years	1	5	22	24	52
		.5%	2.5%	10.0%	5.9%	5.0%
	over 15 years	3	12	3	21	39
		1.5%	6.0%	1.4%	5.1%	3.8%
Total		201	201	221	408	1,031
		100.0%	100.0%	100.0%	100.0%	

Source: Author.

Considering the length of work from home when gender aspects are taken into account for all observed countries together, is shown in Table 3.9.

Table 3.10 confirms that the gender differences in the whole sample are not significant for all countries. Statistical testing was performed via the Mann-Whitney test or Mann—Whitney—Wilcoxon rank-sum test.

The age structure of freelancers shows differences for the analyzed countries (Figure 3.4).

Table 3.9

Length of Work From Home by Gender

	Gender	*N*	Mean Rank	Sum of Ranks
How long have you	Male	547	528.87	289,291.50
Been working from home	Female	484	501.46	242,704.50
	Total	1,031		

Source: Author.

Table 3.10

Mann-Whitney Test [a]

	How long have you been working from home
Mann-Whitney U	125,334.500
Wilcoxon W	242,704.500
Z	–1.910
Asymp. Sig. (2-tailed)	.056

a. Grouping Variable: PolNumeric1.

Figure 3.4.

Age Structure of Freelancers in Serbia, Bosnia and Herzegovina, Montenegro, and Northern Macedonia

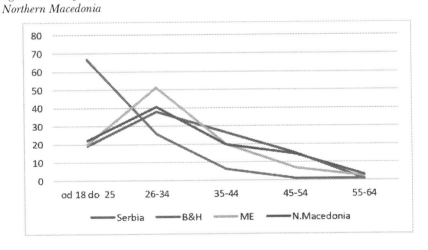

Source: Author.

According to the obtained results, Bosnia and Herzegovina has the most freelancers in the age group from 18–25 (66.7%), while in other countries it is three times lower. This can be explained by the high unemployment rate in Bosnia and Herzegovina, which is the leader in the region.[2] Therefore, most young people as soon as they finish high school (68.8%) in Bosnia and Herzegovina start working in this way.

In Serbia, Montenegro, and Northern Macedonia, in contrast to Bosnia and Herzegovina, the highest percentage of the total number of employees is in the age group of 26–34. Montenegro leads with 50.1%, while in Serbia and Northern Macedonia the percentage is 38 and 40.5%, respectively.

The number of freelancers decreases with the older groups, to be the lowest in the analyzed oldest age group between 55 and 64. Their participation ranges from 0.6 to 3.1%. in Serbia and Northern Macedonia, respectively.

The analysis conducted by the level of education shows that in Serbia, 46.6% of respondents have a high school that operates at distance (whether they are business owners or work from home for employers), while 31.4% are represented with a university degree (Figure 3.5).

Further, in Serbia, almost 90% of respondents who do business from home do so in the field of economics, finance, marketing, and other research, while freelancers 86.2% work in the field of IT and programming. In Northern Macedonia, 81.8% of freelancers also work mostly in the field of IT and programming, while all others who work from home mostly work in the field of industry, 95.7%, followed by transport, 58.3%. In Montenegro, 50% of freelancers work in the IT sector, which is significantly less compared to Serbia and Northern Macedonia. In addition, in Montenegro, 87.5% are mostly those who work from home in the field of services.

The educational structure of freelancers in Serbia is similar to all others who work in some of the ways from home, that is, 50% have completed high school, and 29.5% graduated at faculty (Figure 3.6).

If we compare the educational structure of freelancers in Serbia with other considered countries, the biggest differences are noticed in comparison with Montenegro. Namely, while in Serbia, high school students work mostly as freelancers (50%), in Montenegro, the largest percentage have a university degree (68.9%).

To our question, whether working across platforms and in the "gig economy" can reduce the brain drain abroad, 32.5% of respondents in Bosnia and Herzegovina answered positively, followed by 31.1% of respondents in Serbia and 29.8% in Northern Macedonia. This opinion was least shared by respondents from Montenegro with only 6.6% (Table 3.11).

Figure 3.5

Educational Structure of Self-Employed From Home

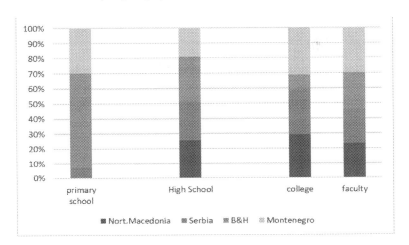

Source: Author.

Figure 3.6

Educational Structure of Freelancers

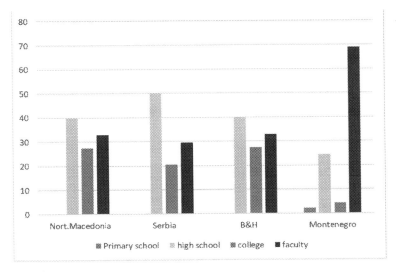

Source: Author.

Table 3.11

Can Working Across Platforms and in the "Gig Economy" Reduce the Brain Drain Abroad?

			Country				
			Bosnia amd Herze-govina	Monte-negro	North-ern Mace-donia	Serbia	Total
Can working across platforms and in the "gig economy" reduce the brain drain abroad?	Yes	Count	94	19	86	90	289
		% within What countrydo you live in?	32.5%	6.6%	29.8%	31.1%	100.0%
		% within What countrydo you live in?	72.9%	42.2%	65.6%	54.2%	61.4%
	No	Count	15	17	5	16	53
		% within What countrydo you live in?	28.3%	32.1%	9.4%	30.2%	100.0%
		% within What countrydo you live in?	11.6%	37.8%	3.8%	9.6%	11.3%
	I do not know	Count	20	9	40	60	129
		% within? What country do you live in?	15.5%	7.0%	31.0%	46.5%	100.0%
		% within? What country do you live in?	15.5%	20.0%	30.5%	36.1%	27.4%

Source: Author.

The significance of these differences was also confirmed by Chi Square Tests (Table 3.12).

To the question, "What are the indicators for determining the success of work from home?", respondents from Serbia and Northern Macedonia (33.3%) answered the same that it was an increase in labor productivity.

Table 3.12

Chi-Square Tests

	Value	df	Asymp. Sig. (2-sided)
Pearson Chi-Square	86.885[a]	18	.000
Likelihood Ratio	87.413	18	.000
Linear-by-Linear Association	43.243	1	.000
N of Valid Cases	471		

a. 9 cells (32.1%) have expected count less than 5. The minimum expected count is .10.

For the respondents from Serbia, the most important indicator of business success from home is higher earnings (48.8%), while for respondents from Bosnia and Herzegovina it was a reduction in business stress (40.5%).

CONCLUSION

Many CEOs and senior managers have changed their minds about remote working equally in a short time. They soon realized that their teams were just as productive from home as they were in the office outside, and some even more productive. As more and more companies adopt remote working policies, working hours are generally adjusted to the employee's schedule and aligned with the employer's requirements. This means, at first glance, greater flexibility and freedom of employees and employers and less stress on both sides (Radović Marković et al., 2021). Namely, there is an opinion that employers should nurture a "flexible organizational culture." In order to build a dynamic team culture at a distance, it is necessary to work on motivating employees to adapt to the common vision and goals of the organization. This in turn encourages collaboration between teams that inspire new ideas and innovations.

The companies that were most willing to accept this modality of work, created a good starting point for the transition to remote working. First of all, they procured software and platforms that were supposed to speed up the digitization of the work process and make it more efficient. To make the most of new software and platforms, employees need to possess the appropriate digital skills. Namely, digital skills are becoming an important prerequisite for employment worldwide, but a significant portion of the population still lacks the skills needed to function in a digital business environment. However, most of them do not actually have enough of these competencies relevant to starting their own entrepreneurial businesses or filling jobs where there is a need for advanced digital skills. Those with the lowest levels of digital skills would be most affected, as well as those who are least willing to upgrade their skills. Accordingly, it is necessary to promote digital entrepreneurial skills and introduce them into education programs through different forms and levels of education.

Our research, which is a pioneering character in this domain when it comes to the countries of the Western Balkans, showed certain specifics of these countries, but also their similarities and differences in terms of remote work. A brief recapitulation of the results showed the following:

- First of all, the respondents from Montenegro were mostly guided by cost savings around renting business premises when choosing to run a home-based business (32.8%), while this factor was the least important for the respondents from Serbia (22.1%).

- For the respondents from Bosnia and Herzegovina, the most important thing to decide to do business from home is the opportunity to balance professional with private and family obligations (39.3%), followed by the respondents from Serbia (29.4%). This factor was of approximate importance for the other two analyzed countries, Montenegro and Bosnia and Herzegovina, that is, about 21%.

- A good business idea was almost equally important for the respondents of Bosnia and Herzegovina (25.4%) and Northern Macedonia (24.4%), while it was the least important for the respondents of Montenegro (18.9%).

- It is interesting that for all countries it was of the least importance to earn extra income among other determining factors to work from home. Thus, only 7.5% of respondents from Montenegro thought that this factor was important for them.

- Serbia has almost 90% of respondents who do business from home in the field of economics, finance, marketing, and other research, while 86.2% of freelancers work in the field of IT and programming.

- What all countries have in common is that employees from home had the highest percentage of experience of 0–5 years.

- The length of work from home by gender did not show significant differences for all observed countries.

- In all countries, an average of 32% of respondents believe that working from home is without working hours, that is, that they work excessively. According to them, this is also one of the great weaknesses of this way of working.

- Bosnia and Herzegovina have the most freelancers in the age group of 18–25 (66.7%), while in other countries the number is three times lower in this group of the working population. In other countries, most freelancers are in the group between the ages of 25–34.
- The number of freelancers decreases with the older groups of the working population, to be the lowest in the analyzed oldest age group between 55 and 64 for all countries.
- In Serbia, high school students work mostly as freelancers (50%), in Montenegro they have the highest percentage of university degrees (68.9%).
- n Serbia, the largest number of respondents believe that a trade union should be established to protect the rights of freelancers (40.9%), while respondents give the least importance to trade unions in this regard (9.7%).
- The respondents in Serbia believe that the adoption of the law on the work of freelancers should provide them with the greatest protection (34.3%), while such an opinion is shared the least by Montenegrins (12%).
- 32.5% of respondents from Bosnia and Herzegovina, followed by 31.1% of respondents from Serbia and 29.8% from Northern Macedonia, thought that working through platforms and in the "gig economy" could reduce the brain drain abroad. The opinion was least shared by the respondents from Montenegro, that is, only 6.6%.
- According to respondents from Serbia and Northern Macedonia, the success of work from home is equally measured by the growth of labor productivity (33.3%). However, for the respondents from Serbia, the most important indicator of business success from home is higher earnings (48.8%), while for the respondents from Bosnia and Herzegovina is a reduction in business stress (40.5%).
- The largest number of respondents do not have a specific business strategy in Montenegro (35.8%), while in other countries this percentage ranged between 24 and 28.7%. Among those who rely on the advice of other experts, it is manifested in Northern Macedonia (29.4%), while this percentage was the lowest in Bosnia and Herzegovina (5.5%).

It can be concluded that our qualitative research results show that a large part of employees in all considered countries accepted remote working relatively well. Also, our research showed that most organizations did not have specific strategies dedicated to remote working. Accordingly, the employees had to adapt to the new situation without any special guide-lines. Despite this, a large number of respondents had a positive attitude towards working from home, considering that remote working gave them the opportunity to better align their responsibilities and be more flexible in time management.

REFERENCES

Allen, J., & Velden, R. (2005). *The flexible professional in the knowledge society: Conceptual framework of the REFLEX.* Maastricht: Research Centre for Education and the Labour Market Maastricht University.

Bang, K. E., & Markeset, T. (2011). Identifying the drivers of economic globalization and the effects on companies' competitive situation, In J. K. Bjørge & T. Laugen (Eds.), *Advances in production management systems. value networks: Innovation, technologies, and management* (pp. 233–241). IFIP WG 5.7 International Conference, APMS 2011, Stavanger, Norway.

Bankar.me. (2019). Retrieved February 20, 2020, from https://www.bankar.me/2019/05/16/turci-u-cg-ulozili-vise-od-165-miliona-eura/

Barrios, S., Holger, G., & Eric, S. (2003), Explaining firms' export behavior: R&D, spillovers and the destination market. *Oxford Bulletin of Economics and Statistics, 65*(4), 475–496.

Barney, J. B. (2007). *Gaining and sustaining competitive advantage.* Pearson Education.

Barth M., Godemann J., Rieckmann M., & Stoltenberg U. (2007) Developing key competencies for sustainable development in higher education. *International Journal of Sustainability in Higher Education, 4*(4), 416–430.

Bartlett, W., & Prica, I. (2017). Interdependence between core and peripheries of the European economy: Secular stagnation and growth in the Western Balkans. *The European Journal of Comparative Economics, 14*(1), 123–139.

Baruch, Y. (2000). Teleworking: benefits and pitfalls as perceived by professionals and managers. *New Technology, Work and Employment, 15*(1), 34–49. https://doi.org/10.1111/1468-005x.00063

Bassellier, G., Benbasat, I., & Reich, B. H. (2003). The influence of business managers IT competence on championing IT. *Information Systems Research, 14*(4), 317–366.

Bana, S. H., Benzell, S. G., & Solares, R. (2020). *Ranking how national economies adapt to remote work.* https://sloanreview.mit.edu/article/ranking-how-national-economies-adapt-to-remote-work/

Bessant, J. , Caffyn, S., & Gallaghe, M. (2001).An evolutionary model of continuous improvement behaviour. *Technovation, 21,* 67–77.

BIZLife. (2020). *Rad od Kuće u Srbiji Utrostručen i Potpuno Neregulisan* [Work from home in Serbia tripled and it is completely unregulated]. https://bizlife.rs/work-from-home-in-serbia-tripled-and-it-is-completely-unregulated/

Bloom, N., & Van Reenen, J., (2002). Patents, real options and firm performance. *The Economic Journal, 112*(478), 97–116.

Bosnia and Herzegovina Agency of Statistics. (2019). www.bhas.ba/?lang=sr

Burke, W. W. (2011). *Organization change: Theory and practice* (3rd ed.). SAGE.

Canto-Sperber, M., & Dupuy, J.-P. (2001). Competencies for the good life and the good society In D. S. Rychen & L. H. Salganik (Eds.), *Defining and selecting key competencies* (pp. 67–92). Hogrefe & Huber.

Central Bank of Montenegro. (2020). Retrieved February 28, 2020, from https://www.paragraf.me/dnevne-vijesti/30012020/30012020-vijest4.html

Digital Serbia. (2020). *Digital 2020: Serbia.* https://datareportal.com/reports/digital-2020-serbia

European Investment Bank. (2019). Retrieved February 1, 2020, from https://www.eib.org/attachments/country/the_eib_in_the_western_balkans_sr.pdf

Employment Agency of Montenegro. (2020). Available at: Statistika–ZZZCG

European Movement of Montenegro. (2013). *Socio-economic position of women in Montenegro.* February 18, 2020, from http://www.emim.org/images/publikacije/socio-ekonomski_polozaj_zena_u_crnoj_gori.pdf

Eurostat. (2019). Employment and unemployment (LFS) – Overview. Available at: Overview – Employment and unemployment (LFS) – Eurostat (europa.eu) (accessed on May 13, 2021)

European Commission. (2018). *Measures in support of a digital agenda for the Western Balkans.* https://www.rcc.int/docs/477/european-commission-measures-in-support-of-a-digital-agenda-for-the-western-balkans

European Commission. (2020). *Srbija pogurala privredni rast Zapadnog Balkana* [Serbia has boosted economic growth in the Western Balkans]. Retrieved February 10, 2020, http://rs.n1info.com/Biznis/a565084/Izvestaj-EK-Srbija-pogurala-privredni-rast-Zapadnog-Balkana.html

European Commission. (2021). *Digital skills and jobs.* https://digital-strategy.ec.europa.eu/en/policies/digital-skills-and-jobs

European Commission. (2021). *Digital Education Action Plan (2021–2027).* https://education.ec.europa.eu/document/digital-education-action-plan

Foss, N. J., & Knudsen, T., (2000). The resource-based tangle: Towards a sustainable explanation of competitive advantage. *Management and Decision Economics, 24*(4), 291–307.

GEM. (2019). KOF index, Global Entrepreneurship Monitor, 2018/2019 Global Report.

Grant, C. A., L. M. Wallace, P. C. Spurgeon, C. Tramontano, & M. Charalampous (2019). Construction and initial validation of the e-Work Life Scale to measure remote e-Working. *Employee Relations, 41*(1), 16–33. https://doi.org/10.1108/ER-09-2017-0229

Global Markets. (2019). *Western Balkans—In business we trust!* Regional Cooperation Council. Retrieved March 6, 2020, frp, https://www.globalcapital.com/Media/documents/emerging-markets/import/Sarajevo_lowres.pdf

Guide to the Europe 2020 Strategy. (2011). *Evropski pokret u Srbiji* [European movement in Serbia]. https://www.emins.org/

Held, D., & McGrew, A., (2007). *Globalization/anti-globalization* (2nd ed.). Wiley.

Helmers, C., & Rogers, M. (2008). Does patenting help high-tech start-ups? (Working Paper). http://www.epip.eu/conferences/epip03/papers/Rogers_HelmersRogersEPIPPatents14092008.pdf

Hitt, M., & He, X. (2008). Firm strategies in a changing global competitive landscape. *Business Horizons, 51*(5), 363–369.

Holmes G., & Hooper N. (2000). Core competence and education. *Higher Education, 40,* 247–258.

Inkpen, A. (1998): Learning, knowledge acquisition, and strategic alliances. *European Management Journal, 16*(2), 223–229.

Jirasavetakul, L. B. F., & J. Rahman. (2018). *Foreign direct investment in new member states of the EU and Western Balkans: Taking stock and assessing prospects* (Working Paper 18/187). International Monetary Fund.

Kasper, G., & Clohesy, S., (2008). *Intentional innovation: How getting more systematic about innovation could improve philanthropy and increase social impact.* W. K. Kellogg Foundation Website. https://www.wkkf.org/resource-directory/resource/2008/09/intentional-innovation-full-report

King, A. W., W., Fowler, S. W., & Zeithaml, C. P. (2001). Managing organizational competencies for competitive advantage: The middle-management edge. *The Academy of Management Executive, 15,* 95–106.

Klette, T. J., & Kortum, S. (2004), Innovating firms and aggregate innovation. *Journal of Political Economy, 112*(5), 986–1018.

Krastev, I. (2018), Europe is facing a potential crisis in the Balkans. It has to act soon. *The Guardian* Retrieved February 21, 2018, from https://www.theguardian.com/commentisfree/2018/feb/21/europe-crisis-balkans-eu-membership-russia-china-turkey

López-Claros, A., & Mata Y. N. (2009). The innovation capacity index: Factors, policies, and institutions driving country innovation. In *The innovation for development report 2009–2010.* Palgrave Macmillan. https://doi.org/10.1057/9780230285477_1

Mahoney, J. T., & Pandian, J. R. (1992). The resource-based view within the conversation of strategic management. *Strategic Management Journal, 13*(5), 363–380.

Ministry of Science of Montenegro. (2019). *Montenegro remains strongly committed to strengthening research infrastructure.* Retrieved February 18 2020, from http://www.mna.gov.me/en/ministry/202541/Montenegro-remains-strongly-committed-to-strengthening-research-infrastructure.html

Mićić, V. (2010). Klasteri–faktor unapređenja konkurentnosti industrije Srbije. *Ekonomski horizonti, 12*(2), 57–74.

Monstat. (2019). *Statistical yearbook—Tourism.* Retrieved March 6, 2020, from http://www.monstat.org/userfiles/file/publikacije/godisnjak%202019/18.pdf

Montenegro tourism development strategy to 2020. (2008). *Montenegro Ministry of Tourism and Environment.* https://www.gov.me/dokumenta/9b158c2a-90d8-46bf-92e6-9374d4b7a24b

National Council for Scientific and Technological Development of the Republic of Serbia. (2018). *The position of science in Serbia* (Working Paper).

National Development Strategy of Montenegro 2008–2030 (2007). *Ministry of Sustainable development and Tourism.* https://sustainabledevelopment.un.org/memberstates/montenegro

New Economy. (2020). *Turske investicije u Srbiji: Rast u turbulentnim vremenima* [Turske investicije u Srbiji: Rast u turbulentnim vremenima]. Retrieved February 25, 2020, from https://novaekonomija.rs/vesti-iz-zemlje/turske-investicije-u-srbiji-rast-u-turbulentnim-vremenima

Official Gazette of the Republic of Serbia. (2016, November 24). Retrieved February 20, 2021, from r4.pdf (mtt.gov.rs)

Official Gazette of Montenegro. (2018). No. 42/16) 27.

Organisation for Economic Co-operation and Development (OECD). (2018). *Multinational enterprises in the global economy: Heavily debated but hardly measured* (May Policy Note). Retrieved February 5, 2020, from https://www.oecd.org/industry/ind/MNEs-in the-global-economy-policy-note.pdf

Organisation for Economic Co-operation and Development. (2010). *Recommendation of the Council on Information and Communication Technologies and the Environment.*

Pascoe, K. (2019). *What's the difference between being freelance and self-employed?* https://medium.com/the-post-grad-survival-guide/whats-the-difference-between-being-freelance-and-self-employed-f2bd6766d4cd

Pavlova, I. (2020). *SEE GDP to drop 2.5% in 2020 over coronavirus—RBI.* Retrieved March 25, 2020, from https://seenews.com/news/see-gdp-to-drop-25-in-2020-over-coronavirus-rbi-691457

Pucko, D. (1998). Researching management in Central and Eastern Europe: Researcher, manager and management practice. Comment and views, Journal for East European Management Studies, ISSN 0949-6181. *Rainer Hampp Verlag, Mering, 3*(3), 290–293.

Radović-Marković, M. (2011). Uticaj globalizacije na stvaranje novog modela preduzeća i njegovih konkurentnih prednosti, Radno-pravni savetnik, Poslovni biro, Beograd [The impact of globalization on the creation of a new company model and its competitive advantages, Labor and Legal Advisor, Business Bureau, Belgrade].

Radović-Marković, M. (2011a). Obrazovni sistem i potrebe privrede u srbiji, pogl. U knjizi, AKTIVNE MERE NA TRŽIŠTU RADA I PITANJA ZAPOSLENOSTI (ur.Jovan Zubović), Institut ekonomskih nauka, Beograd [Education system and needs of the economy in Serbia, ch. In the book, ACTIVE MEASURES ON THE LABOR MARKET AND EMPLOYMENT ISSUES (ed. Jovan Zubović), Institute of Economic Sciences, Belgrade].

Radović Marković, M., & Tomaš, R. (2019). *Globalization and entrepreneurship in small countries.* Routledge.

Radović-Marković, M. (2019a). Jačanje naučne saradnje u oblasti društvenih i ekonomskih nauka izmedju Sjedinjenih Američkih Država i Srbije, Filozofski fakultet (grupa za istoriju) i Institut ekonomskih nauka, Beograd [Strengthening scientific cooperation in the field of social and economic sciences between the United States and Serbia, Faculty of Philosophy (History Group) and Institute of Economic Sciences].

Radović Marković, M., & Đukanović, B., Marković, D., & Dragojević, A., (2021). *Entrepreneurship and work in the gig economy—The case of the Western Balkans.* Routledge.

Radović-Marković, M., Grozdanić, R., & Jevtić, B. (2013). *Private sector development in the Western Balkans compared to the EU countries.* Institiute of Economic Sciences, Belgrade, Serbia.

Report of the National Science Council of the Republic of Serbia. (2018). Working Paper.

Reporting Democracy. (2020). *Hungary's Green Fund for Western Balkans a 'Win-Win'.* Retrieved April 15, 2020, from https://balkaninsight.com/2020/03/11/hungarys-green-fund-for-western-balkans-a-win-win/

Rockart, J. F., Earl, M. J., & Ross, J. W. (1996). Eight imperatives for the new IT organization. *Sloan Management Review, 38*(1), 43–55.

Ross, S. (2020). *Developing countries lose out due to low prevalence of remote working jobs—Leading macroeconomic influencers.* https://www.pharmaceutical-technology.com/features/low-prevalence-remote-working/

SEE. (2020). South East Europe 2020 strategy. Retrieved January 19, 2020, from https://wbc-rti.info/object/document/14428

Statistic Times. (2019). http://statisticstimes.com/ranking/global-innovation-index.php

SJR. (2018). *Scimago Journal & Country Rank.* Retrieved March 17, 2020, from https://www.scimagojr.com/countryrank.php?region=Eastern%20Europe&year=2018

Statistic Times. (2019). Retrieved March 11, 2020, from http://statisticstimes.com/ranking/global-innovation-index.php

Sullivan, S. E., & Baruch, Y. (2009). Advances in career theory and research: A critical review and agenda for future exploration. *Journal of Management, 35*(6), 1542–1571.

Tippins, M. J., & Sohi, R. S. (2003). IT competency and firm performance: Is organizational learning a missing link? *Strategic Management Journal, 24,* 745–761.

Tekin, H., & Tekdogana, O. F. (2015). Socio-cultural dimension of innovation, *Procedia—Social and Behavioral Sciences, 195,* 1417–1424.

Tomchev, P. (2017). *China's road: Into the Western Balkans.* https://www.iss.europa.eu/sites/default/files/EUISSFiles/Brief%203%20China%27s%20Silk%20Road.pdf

Trading Economics. (2020). *Serbia unemployment rate.* Retrieved March 12, 2020, from https://tradingeconomics.com/serbia/unemployment-rate

UNCTAD. (2019), *World investment report.* Retrieved April 10, 2020, from https://unctad.org/en/PublicationsLibrary/wir2019_en.pdf

World Economic Forum. (2019). *The global competitiveness index 2019.* Retrieved March 12, 2021, from http://www3.weforum.org/docs/WEF_TheGlobalCompetitivenessReport2019.pdf

World Economic Forum. (2019a). http://www3.weforum.org/docs/WEF_TTCR_2019.pdf

World Economic Forum. (2020). *This is how the Western Balkans will become more innovative.* Retrieved March 13, 2020, from https://www.weforum.org/agenda/2020/02/western-balkans-become-more-innovative/

World Bank. (2019). *Western Balkans regular economic report: Fall 2019*. Retrieved March 1, 2020, from https://www.worldbank.org/en/region/eca/publication/western-balkans-regular-economic-report

World Bank. (2019a). *Tržište rada na Zapadnom Balkanu beleži bolje rezultate, ali ostaju problemi vezani za žene, mlade i manje obrazovane radnike* [The Western Balkans labor market is performing better, but problems remain for women, young and less educated workers]. Retrieved March 10, 2020, from https://www.worldbank.org/sr/news/press-release/2019/03/19/western-balkans-show-improved-labor-market-performance-but-challenges-remain-for-women-youth-and-less-educated-workers

World Bank. (2019b). *Migration and brain drain*. Retrieved March 19, 2020, from https://thedocs.worldbank.org/en/doc/657841579634335146-0080022020/original/October2019ECAResearchNotesMigrationandBrainDrain.pdf

World Bank. (2019d). *Redovni Ekonomski Izveštaj Za Zapadni Balkan Br. 16* [Regular economic report for the Western Balkans No. 16]. Retrieved March 1, 2020, from http://pubdocs.worldbank.org/en/974781570527082774/WBRER16-SRB.pdf

World Bank. (2020). *Global economic prospects*. Retrieved March 10, 2020, from https://www.worldbank.org/en/publication/global-economic-prospects

Vladimirov, M., Kovačević, M., Mirjacic, M., Novakovic, I., Štiplija, N., Nuredinoska, E., & Dimiškova, S. (2018). *Russian economic footprint in the Western Balkans. Corruption and state capture risks*. Center for the Study of Democracy. https://csd.bg/publications/publication/russian-economic-footprint-in-the-western-balkans-corruption-and-state-capture-risks/

Vučeković, M., Medić, Z., & Marković, D. (2020). E-learning for entrepreneurial skills in a digital business environment. *International Review, 2020*(1–2), 27–33. Retrieved May 17, 2021, from https://www.researchgate.net/publication/344599692_E-learning_for_entrepreneurial_skills_in_a_digital_business_environment

Zack, M. H. (1999). Developing a knowledge strategy. *California Management Review, 41*(3), 125–145.

ZUNS. (2019). *Ulaganje u Nauku I Dalje Nedovoljno* [Investing in science and further insufficient]. Podgorica. Retrieved March 12, 2020, from https://www.zuns.me/prosvjetni-rad/clanak/ministarka-nauke-sanja-damjanović-ulaganje-u-nauku-i-dalje-nedovoljno

Zupan, N. (1996). Human resources as a source of competitive advantage in transitional companies: The vase of Slovenia. *Slovenska Ekonomska Revija*, [Slovenian Economic Review], *47*(5–6), 510–524.

NOTES

1. Appendix contains the questionnaires used for the research.
2. See Chapter 1.

PART II

SOCIOPSYCHOLOGICAL ASPECTS OF NEW MODALITIES OF WORK

CHAPTER 4

COVID-19 AND REMOTE WORK IN WESTERN BALKANS

Sociopsychological Impact

Borislav Đjukanović

INTRODUCTION

Remote work includes many manifestations having one common feature of the employee performing it outside the employer's workplace with the application of modern information and communication technologies. In everything else, there are numerous differences and specifics, both in terms of time and place of work, legal regulations, employment status, the ability to work as a freelancer for one or more employers at the same time. In particular, the relationships of the self-employed who work remotely are complex. These are all reasons to find a common denominator for all these different manifestations in the development of our research design as much as possible, which was very difficult, if not impossible. Nevertheless, we have adapted the content of our research instruments to this basic endeavor.

Macroeconomics of Western Balkans in the Context of the Global Work and Business Environment, pp. 63–154
Copyright © 2022 by Information Age Publishing
www.infoagepub.com

The first assumption that we would succeed in this regard is the reduction of all relevant research indicators to certain more general categories, which inevitably leads to certain simplifications.

These simplifications are reinforced by a very wide coverage of different psychosocial, economic aspects and freelancers. The generalization of the researched phenomena into basic forms also occurred due to the need for a very rational and economical conduct of electronic surveying, which for each of the three types of questionnaires were reduced to 15 questions. Namely, with great difficulty, we managed to collect data for three questionnaires for each of the 1,031 respondents. Our personal very modest financial resources were also a limiting factor.

Since this is exploratory research, we have set research goals more as analytical guidelines than they arise from a stronger theoretical—hypothetical basis. We did not find similar research in either domestic or foreign research.

Given the broadly set research design, our intention is primarily to point out the basic tendencies.

Conditionally, our first goal is to describe the psychosocial problems raised by respondents in four countries.

The second goal is to determine the similarities and differences in the manifestation of psychosocial problems among respondents from four countries.

The third goal is to describe the economic advantages and disadvantages presented by respondents from four countries and to identify similarities and differences in this regard among them.

The fourth goal is freelancing in four countries—pointing out the similarities and differences among freelancers in those countries. Based on the obtained results, we will describe the social profiles of respondents who work from home in each country, and then point out the differences and similarities. Finally, we will try to "reconstruct" a general common profile.

LITERATURE REVIEW

Research on remote work is polarized in two basic directions. The focus of the first direction's interests is on the various psychosocial problems that people who work at home have, while the second is predominantly oriented towards the benefits that individuals and work organizations have from remote work, especially in terms of productivity and savings. We will deal with both.

Positive and negative factors of working from home are:

The positive

- Flexibility of work

- Increased autonomy and self-confidence
- Better planning of work and private commitments
- Reduced stress due to better concentration and fewer job-related mistakes
- Increased motivation
- Increased productivity
- Reduction of utility and lease costs
- Reduction of transportation costs
- Improving the health status
- Increased job satisfaction
- Higher earnings
- Reduced absences and sick leave
- Greater time savings
- Greater employment opportunities for the disabled and handicapped
- Savings on business lunches and dressing-up

The negative

- Loss of boundaries between work and family
- Poor communication due to poor feedback
- Loss of face-to-face contact with colleagues
- Lack of connection with management
- Staying at work much longer than working hours
- Constant tension due to work overload
- Lack of technical support from management
- Lack of social support from work colleagues
- Lack of social support from family members, friends, and neighbors
- Feelings of marginalization from employers
- The feeling that superiors do not know and do not follow our real contributions
- The belief that we are forgotten when it comes to professional advancement, earnings, etc.
- Poor professional identification with the company

From the introductory remarks, it could be concluded that remote work has a number of positive effects, which is why it is constantly increasing in most countries, although this speed depends on a number of technological, economic, sociopolitical, and cultural characteristics of a particular country. Remote work has allowed much greater flexibility, which is associated with increased company productivity, reduced travel costs and time, reduced absenteeism and increased traffic, improved employee health and job satisfaction (Allen, 2001; Baltes et al., 1999; Gajendran & Harisson, 2007; Greenhaus & Powell, 2006; Kurland & Bailey, 1999; Thomas & Ganster, 1995).

In countries where quarantine is applied due to the COVID-19 pandemic, the only option is to work from home. However, when there was no pandemic, some companies preferred working from home for several reasons:

- Reduced costs of companies are mentioned first, such as renting office space, maintenance, computers, telephones, utilities, equipment, and so forth (Lupu, 2017). Some offices avoid leasing for additional offices through remote management programs, and also because of employee parking costs (Beňo, 2018).

Due to increased motivation, worker productivity has also increased (Lupu, 2017). Why has productivity increased? At home, workers have long periods of uninterrupted time on the same tasks, without intrusions and interruptions, resulting in increased motivation, increased satisfaction, and better employee commitment to work at home. Working energy is increased and hindering factors are reduced to a minimum.

Regardless of the COVID-19 pandemic, working from home was the best, if not the only, option for certain categories. This primarily refers to the disabled, mothers with children, people who live very far from the office and do not want to move (Ford & Butts, 1991).

Certain categories of employees for a number of reasons are faced with numerous absences (due to chronic diseases, sick children, sick elderly relatives, infectious diseases, etc.).

Reducing the spread of infectious diseases among employees is also one of the important benefits of working from home.

Finally, working from home has been shown to reduce occupational stress, decreased concentration, and work-related errors.

New modalities of work contain two important determinants: they are supported by new information and communication technologies and have clearly defined goals (Nijp et al., 2016). The advantages of digitalization are that the work can be done in different spatial and temporal frameworks and replace face-to-face relationships. Digitization significantly reduces costs, leads to time savings, and improves the quality of the environment (Demerouti et al., 2014).

There are a number of benefits for employers who introduce remote work: increased satisfaction and productivity, reduced geographical constraints, greater choice of skilled labor, and increased trust among employer and employees (Baruch, 2000; Morgan, 2004). When it comes to the employee, then the prerequisites for efficient work are self-motivation, integrity, self-confidence, and good communication skills (Baruch, 2000; Morgan, 2004).

Adequate supervision and support of employees, adequate managerial training with the application of good formal and informal communication skills are important for efficient and successful remote work (Kowalski & Swanson, 2005). Employees need to have clear expectations about remote work, and therefore training is needed when it comes to the boundaries between work and private life (Kowalski & Swanson, 2005). All of this needs to be precisely and clearly defined in the psychological contract (Morgan, 2004). However, there are not many remote work training programs (Clear & Dickson, 2005).

What benefits are most often highlighted in remote work: better work-life balance, increased flexibility, reduction of commuting, reduced overhead costs for the employer, better basis for developing skills for the employer, increased productivity and so forth (Jensen, 1994; Mann et al., 2000; Montreuil & Lippel, 2003)

- Flexible working hours

Probably the most important motive for working at home is flexible working hours (Lupu, 2017). Thanks to that, the employee gains a certain autonomy because he can distribute business and private obligations according to his own needs and daily planning. Employees can change their work schedule on a daily basis or even make hourly changes (Ford & Butts, 1991). Advantages of flexible working hours: if it suits them, they can finish work late, sleeping in the morning until they want, without feeling greater external pressures of working for 10 hours during the week (Wienclaw, 2019). Appointments for the performance of various private duties can be made during working hours, without taking days off, which was not the case when working in the office. The advantage is the great saving of time and nerves when leaving and arriving from work during the biggest traffic jams, which are quite stressful. In that way, stress is avoided and with all that, you get a lot of free time that you can spend with your family.

The flexibility provided by working from home is needed by people for a number of reasons. The authors highlight the key benefits of working from home such as easier doing the chores (Wheatley, 2017) especially in families with children (Vilhelmson & Thulin, 2016). Over time, autonomy also strengthens. All of these processes result in increased motivation and job satisfaction, conditioned by better job control and working time flexibility (Binder & Coad, 2016; Felstead & Henseke, 2017; Hill et al., 2003; Wheatley, 2017). In the following study, the authors first point out the advantages of remote work: better work-life balance, increased flexibility, reduced commuting, reduced overhead costs for the employer, better basis for developing skills for the employer, increased productivity, and more (Jensen, 1994; Mann et al., 2000; Montreuil & Lippel, 2003). The main challenge for working from home is the opportunity to find a better balance between business and private life. Financial savings are also significant because they do not travel to work, including gasoline, vehicle depreciation, and parking costs (Wienclaw, 2019). It also saves on lunches at work, special clothing, and so forth. We have already mentioned that financial savings and stress reduction are greatest for the disabled, the handicapped, those who live very far away and do not have the funds to rent an apartment near the office. In addition, home workers can provide help to sick children or the elderly with a flexible schedule of business and other obligations, if they need help (Beňo, 2018).

In a sample of 30,000 households in the United Kingdom, it was found that the growth of satisfaction due to work at home is conditioned by the increase in free time (Reuschke, 2019).

Working from home is favored; 85% of job seekers would be more likely to stay with the employer who would occasionally provide them with a flexible job (Twentyman, 2010). Others report a high level of job satisfaction associated with flexible working hours that allows for good planning to gain plenty of free time for other activities (Madsen, 2011; Wheatley, 2012).

Valuing good and bad jobs from home primarily comes down to the issue of a good balance between business and private life, for which it is especially important to have flexible working hours. Meeting these challenges is achieved through nonstandard working time arrangements, in which employees work outside working hours during the working week (Krahn, 1995; Li et al., 2014; Stone, 2012). Imbalance of work and family life affects the health of other family members (Li et al., 2014). The phenomenon of burnout at work due to overwork (Cassells et al., 2011; Williams et al., 2008) especially highlights the importance of distinguishing between good and bad work at home. In relation to the numerous work engagements in time and space that enables flexible working hours, working longer than full-time work in long periods of time is certainly the most unfavorable effect on family and private life.

It should be noted that probably many, who decided to work from home, already showed tendencies for autonomy in work and preferred a free schedule of work activities during the day).

They find it easier to establish boundaries between work and private life (Kreiner et al., 2009) owing to increased self-discipline, self-motivation and efficient scheduling and completion of business tasks (Richardson & McKenna, 2014). It would be very interesting in one longitudinal study to examine how much the mentioned positive personality traits dictate later commitment to work from home and how much on the basis of such personality traits these tendencies towards greater self-discipline, self-motivation and efficient planning and execution of daily tasks develop. We are aware that such research is very difficult to report due to large methodological and other requirements and limitations, but it would be useful to realize it at least in segments.

Of the negative aspects, social isolation stands out (Fonner & Roloff; 2012; Pinsonneault & Boisvert, 2001) as well as the problem of exclusion from work (Felstead & Henseke, 2017). Young children create special difficulties for working at home (Pinsonneault & Boisvert, 2001) and constant interruptions during work by family members, friends, and neighbors (Gurstein, 1996).

Working from home is invisible to employers, which affects the occurrence of discomfort and fear among employees that they will lack the expected praise, salary increases, and promotions (Cooper & Kurland, 2002).

Productivity

Of all the aspects of remote work, the greatest attention is paid to productivity. It is viewed in the context of very different positive and negative factors. In this study, the authors deal with work processes from home that lead to increased work effort and productivity. Their basic conclusion is that working from home leads to an increase in work effort and employee productivity (Rupietta & Beckmann, 2016). In 2012, more than 20% of German companies allow employees to work from home for a few days a month (Flüter-Hoffmann, 2012). It has been noticed that employees who work from home increase their autonomy in scheduling and organizing their work. Employees with greater autonomy are much more motivated to put in the extra effort. This also explains increased productivity (Baily & Kurland, 2002; Bailyn, 1988; DuBrin, 1991; Hackman & Oldman, 1976; Olson, 1989,). Recent research has shown that there is no simple linear relationship between work from home, motivation, and productivity; productivity increases if tasks at work are creative and decreases if they are not creative (Bloom et al., 2015; Dutcher, 2012).

Unlike all these studies, even those based on laboratory or field experiments, the conclusions of this study (Rupietta & Beckman, 2016) are based on representative data (socioeconomic panel) and the conclusions of the study are highly representative.

Twenty-two thousand individuals in 12,000 households were included. The main result is that employees who often work from home show more work effort than those who rarely work from home or work constantly in the office. Increased work effort strengthens motivation and productivity, and by increasing motivation and productivity, work effort also strengthens. A kind of closed circle is created. This leads to a paradoxical twist that employers misinterpret: employees who show increased work effort during unpaid overtime and have a more positive attitude towards work and greater motivation than those who are paid overtime. The conclusion is clear; working from home strengthens autonomy, motivation and work effort despite the fact that many overtime unpaid hours remain invisible to employers. Previously, employers believed that working outside the work organization provided an opportunity to relax, slack off, or engage in private jobs. This and other previously mentioned studies show just the opposite; working from home is a very good way to boost intrinsic motivation, work effort and, consequently, productivity. That is why German companies are increasingly turning to work from home, while respecting all the specifics shown by the results of this and other mentioned studies.

In one very important study, the authors performed a comparative analysis of five representative studies of the same groups of factors that had a positive or negative effect on productivity in 2000 and five representative studies between 2019 and 2020 (Thorstensson, 2020). The result of the comparative analysis is that some factors act positively, some negatively, while the influence of some depends on the attitudes of employees and a combination of other circumstances.

One of the key factors is the organization's policy towards those who work from home. Productivity increases if employees feel that their company trusts and cares for them, providing them with adequate training, if they organize their work well and adequately allocate resources to get the job done on time. Adequate workspace is also important, which allows them to be fully focused on work without disturbing others. Lack of face-to-face communication often has a negative effect on productivity. It is important that there is no delay in information when it comes to teamwork, and it is especially important that there is no high level of data interdependence, which causes delays and waiting in some links of the chain. Working from home for a long time causes a feeling of social and professional isolation and disconnection, which affects the decline in productivity. It is interesting to note that video calls increase productivity more than email and messaging because video calls simulate face-to-face contact.

Working from home largely depends on technical support. If employees have good access to certain technologies, equipment and tools, good technical and logistical support, productivity increases, and if the internet is weak or interrupted, if the power grid is weak, there are difficulties in sending data among employees and productivity falls.

Certainly, productivity depends on the personal characteristics of employees at home, but also on the specific circumstances. We have already emphasized the importance of flexible working hours. Whether it will increase or decrease productivity depends on the person. If employees at home do not have working time restrictions and can freely determine the place and time of work, it is important that they have self-discipline and self-efficiency, time management skills, ability, will and inner motivation to work remotely. Such a constellation of positive factors will certainly increase productivity. If the employee does not have the necessary discipline and motivation, but only reacts to external pressures, his productivity will drastically decrease. If employees perceive the home as a comfortable place to relax and rest and if they are tempted to play video games, access social networks, watch movies, and so forth, their productivity will inevitably be low.

The productivity of those who work from home is affected by technical problems that cannot be solved remotely, the inequality of salaries of those who work remotely and those who work from the office, the lack of employer insight into increased work effort and significantly longer average working hours of remote workers. Further, the isolation of employees at home and the lack of confirmation from colleagues about efficiency and success in work, the lack of direct interactions with colleagues during and after work reduces productivity. Remote employees feel forgotten especially when it comes to job advancement because in a way their work becomes less visible to everyone simply because great physical distance creates barriers to the work environment. The values and goals of the company to the remote worker also become unclear and distant (Ford & Butts, 1991). Such a status also affects their future employment, as new employers doubt the recommendations of the current ones because their perception is often unclear. The current employer simply knows little about the social and other skills of those who work remotely. Individually or cumulatively, such a climate does not contribute to productivity growth.

Consequently, organizations fear that employees from home may lose control and connection to the organization. They fear that remote workers may give preference to personal jobs or work for others, which can reduce not only productivity but also the quality of work, regardless of all established control mechanisms using new technical devices (Peeters et al., 2005). Moving away from superiors and office colleagues can eventually lead to a loss of identity with the company and a loss of team spirit in the work.

In the further analysis of this exceptional work (Thorstensson, 2020), the author dealt with the determination of similarities and differences in positive and negative factors in 2000 and 2019–2020. Basically, she pointed out more similarities than differences. While in 2000, access to certain equipment, technology and appropriate tools was important to increase productivity in 2020, it is no longer because that approach is simply implied for everyone who works from home. We mentioned that there is one factor that increases productivity, and that is video calls instead of e-mails. It should be borne in mind that video calls in 2000 did not exist. The smartphones and social networks we mentioned in a negative context to increase productivity in 2000 were not common, so this comparison is also not relevant.

Nevertheless, psychological factors are key to the decline in productivity. The first is the great fear of infection. The second is the feeling of social disconnection and isolation from the work environment with at the same time increased tensions and conflicts within the family due to forced isolation for a long time. At the same time, due to isolation, earlier assistance to the family for the care of children and the elderly is lacking (Baines & Gelder, 2003; Sullivan, 2012; Weinert et al., 2015). All these objective circumstances make it very difficult to establish clear boundaries between business and private life and affect the reduction of productivity.

An Indonesian study (Susilo et al., 2020) points out that a pleasant work environment is key to successful telecommuting and increased productivity.

If it is known that Indonesia has 136 million total employees (Susilo et al, 2020), this knowledge will undoubtedly be useful. However, in this study, as in most other, no control variables were introduced that could significantly affect the results, such as: gender, age, education, cultural patterns, adopted technologies, types of industry, stratum affiliation, income level, and so forth.

Issues of productivity at work from home are relativized not only because of the controlling variables but also by the very value determinations of good and bad work from home. Individuals who work from home are often unable to limit working hours for a variety of reasons—fears that the employer will not like them enough and therefore will not keep the job in the long run, that they may earn more by working overtime and thus achieve their excessive ambitions and expectations or that they see overtime as the only way to meet different external pressures and expectations. Unable to establish self-discipline and respond assertively to all external and internal pressures, many are obsessively attached to work, dependent on work, which leads to burnout and numerous disturbances in family life. As a confirmation of this compulsive attitude towards work, the satisfaction they achieve between the time spent at work and the desired time is more important for most than the number of hours worked (Wooden et al., 2009). Poor productivity is just one and not the most devastating consequence. That is why the most important decision for all those who work remotely is to find a good balance between private life and professional obligations, which is certainly the biggest and most difficult enigma that many who work from home fail to solve.

One should not lose sight of many employees working remotely being imperceptibly drawn into relationships that are more promising than fulfilling. A good example of this is internet gigs (Graham et al., 2017). In the global virtual labor market, Internet gigs for middle- and lower-income workers are becoming the main source of monthly funding and increasing workers' autonomy, which is why this market is growing rapidly. However, it is often associated with a series of traps into which participants are drawn beyond their will and expectations. The loss of the boundaries between work and private life is an epiphenomenon of a series of negative phenomena of those who participate in internet gigs. In one large survey, 55% of respondents worked at high speed compared to only 13% who did not, and only 15% of respondents did not have too short deadlines to complete work, while 22% experienced pain due to such short deadlines. This intensity of work was accompanied by low wages, job insecurity. The main way to increase wages was by increasing the number of working hours. Some said they would work 70–80 hours a week for a salary of $ 3.5 an hour, and sometimes all night if deadlines were tight (Graham et al., 2017). As many as 70% stated that they know very little about their clients, and that they do not have a clear or acceptable tax policy. In addition, most point out that they are exposed to extreme predation and exploitation of intermediaries. In practice, they cannot easily exercise their rights, and are often discriminated against in a subtle and sometimes open way (Graham et al., 2017).

Lithuania's experience in various aspects of remote working is valuable because it took place in almost experimental conditions; four years ago, in terms of the number of those working remotely, it was on the European backlog, so that during the COVID-19 pandemic, as many as 40% of employees worked remotely.

Remote work has made it possible to adapt to market changes and crises, such as COVID-19 (Bhat et al., 2017; Großer & Baumöl, 2017). The consulting companies pay special attention to maintaining and increasing productivity (Bouziri et al., 2020; Raghuram et al. 2019) as well as establishing a balance between work from home and private life (Čulo, 2016; Verburg et al., 2013). On this occasion, we should mention the instructive and precise definition of a virtual organization given by the authors: "A virtual organization is a collection of geographically distributed, functionally or culturally diverse entities that are connected by electronic forms of communication and use electronic media to communicate, coordinate and fulfil the defined goal or task" (Stachova et al., 2018)

- Leadership in remote working

In the introductory part of this study, the authors pay special attention to leadership in virtual teams, related to communication and trust issues (Baert et al., 2020; Brynjolfsson, 2020; Cogliser, 2012; Daim et al., 2012; Ospina, 2017; Taylor, 2018). In order to form communication rules, motivate employees for calm, continuous communication based on the feelings, attitudes and behaviors of employees, to achieve fast and efficient exchange of information in virtual teams it is necessary to have a strong leader (Kuscu & Hasan, 2014; Snellman, 2014). There is a general belief that it is much easier to be a leader in traditional than digital teams because in working on platforms, individuals are leaders themselves. Working on the platforms establishes cooperation and trust that abolish the privileges and powers of leaders, stimulating employees to take the lead on their own, which leads to a large number of remote workers participating in the leadership. Such shared leadership encourages motivation, coordination, and efficiency (Arnfalk, 2016). Some authors equate leadership in digital organizations with collective leadership that cooperates effectively and makes good decisions (Baert et al., 2020; Brynjolfsson, 2020).

Comparison of work from home and office

In the following study, researchers address the advantages and disadvantages of working from home and from the office of teaching and research staff in Hungary (Aczel et al., 2021). The mentioned research of advantages and disadvantages of work from the house of scientists is quite rare and in some aspects unexpected, and on this occasion we will present the basic results (Aczel et al., 2021)

Comparing the results of work from home and in the office during the pandemic, they said that they exchange information with colleagues more successfully in the office and prepare data collection tasks more efficiently, and prepare manuscripts, follow literature, and analyze data more successfully at home.

It was a particularly interesting question about how much time they spent in the past and how much they would need in the future to achieve optimal results with which they would be satisfied.

To achieve the required efficiency, as many as 66% said they should work more from home than they did before the pandemic, 16% want less, and 18% the same time as before the pandemic. Finally, 86% of all scientists, who said that they would work more from home in the future, believe that working from home would be an ideal and possible solution.

Contrary to previous beliefs that working from home has particularly affected the academic community and has significantly reduced the quality and productivity of their work, this research has shown that the academic community fits very well into the processes associated with new forms of work and the information and communication technologies that support them, so that working from home is supported by the majority as an ideal solution in the future. Truth be told, some forms of work are realized more effectively by members of the academic community in direct communication with colleagues, primarily related to the exchange of ideas in planning and implementation of scientific projects, but two thirds would like to work from home than before the pandemic.

However, in order to realize the preferences of academic staff for increased work from home in the future, the authors of this paper justifiably suggest that they need social help and support in those aspects that hinder or limit their work from home now, and certainly in the future.

The biggest problem is caring for children, regardless of the fact that working from home enables them to take care of children more. However, caring for children is for them the main reason for overload and the main source of conflict between work and family (Adkins & Premeaux, 2012; Premeaux et al., 2007), which is why employers need help in this area when it comes to children, and other categories that require special care, such as the elderly and the disabled (Eikhof et al., 2007). Remediation should also include addressing a range of adverse family circumstances, including the challenges of single life.

- Balance and boundaries between work and private life

Given that scientists in the future prefer to work from home, the authors rightly conclude that between work and private life they will have more and more problems to connect work and private life in this context (Aczel et al., 2021).

The reasons for the conflict are the demands of certain roles that try to provide someone's mental and physical capacities in order to be realized, so that the borders easily weaken and the private enters the business field and vice versa. The consequences are weaker concentration at work and exhaustion (Golden, 2012; Kim & Holenbe, 2017) and reduced job satisfaction (Carlson et al., 2010).

Traditional boundaries between work and private life have broken down, and new ones, which would be appropriate for new information and communication technologies, have not been built. Scientists adapt to them in accordance with external constraints, internal needs and requirements, so that they more or less successfully use different ways and means to establish and maintain borders.

Many of the relevant factors that may influence the maintenance or permeability of borders in one direction or another have not been sufficiently examined and clarified. In any case, there are a number of challenges for future researchers to come to more reliable conclusions.

At least in the ideal projection, the solution lies in the acceptance of boundary theory. According to this theory, people use different tactics to maintain an ideal level of segmentation of work from home (Ashforth et al., 2000; Clark, 2000). Those who have built-in preferences and tactics for managing borders manage borders more strictly and develop strong segmentation between work and family (Nippert-Eng, 1996).

A study by Grant et al. (2013) considers three aspects of working from home: efficiency, well-being, and the distinction between work and private life. In addition to numerous savings, working from home provides opportunities for the individual to best balance the relationship between business and private life (Lewis & Cooper, 2005). When the boundaries between work and private life weaken or collapse, there are numerous negative consequences. Then the positive effects such as reducing stress and increasing satisfaction disappear, and most of the protective elements weaken and disappear when working from home (Hartig et al., 2007). The collapse of borders can lead to completely opposite effects: increased stress, family conflicts and lack of free time. Despite the fact that working from home can increase satisfaction and productivity while reducing absenteeism, conflicts in the family due to the intertwining of business and private life can remain and form the other side of the coin (Allvin et al., 2011; Noonan & Glass, 2012).

The blurring of the boundaries between work and family generates many other problems, which 60% of workers in one study cite as the dominant problem (Ellison, 1999).

Working from home generates a number of problems when there is no balance between work and private life because the boundaries are blurred, confusing (Demerouti et al., 2014). Conflict between work and family is considered to be the most important for the occurrence of burnout (Dyrbye et al., 2011; Lingard & Francis, 2006).

A study of 1,500 respondents found that gender aspects and the presence of a dependent did not have a particular impact on work efficiency, but the ability to manage working hours was the most important determinant of maintaining work-life balance (Maruyama et al., 2009).

COMPARISON OF WORKING FROM HOME BEFORE AND AFTER THE COVID-19 PANDEMIC

From the following study (Graham et al., 2017), we would also like to single out the findings related to the comparison of the perception of working of those who first started working remotely and those who have experience of remote work before the COVID-19. Those who started during the pandemic emphasize the shortcomings less, but also emphasize the positive aspects of remote work. Those who worked before the pandemic highlighted the negative aspects of this work, such as lack of face-to-face communication with managers, difficulties in accessing job-related information, lack of feedback, overtime due to managerial pressures, inability to adequately assess workload, belief that the supervisor inadequately evaluates their work, and so forth. They pointed out mostly the negative aspects of remote work, with their work motivation being quite low.

Respondents who have longer experience with remote work have described both the pros and cons of this chapter in much more detail. The positive aspects were mainly related to the flexibility of work organization, choice of place and time of work, savings, and so forth. The negative ones were related to limitations and career insecurity, long-lasting and complicated communication processes. Finally, those who worked only two days a week remotely had more positive attitudes about this work than those who worked full time; those who worked only two days emphasized the benefits more, and those who worked three days or full time emphasized the disadvantages more. It should be mentioned that the elderly are generally more critical of remote work.

In a recent longitudinal study in the United Kingdom, which offers a number of interesting results on this topic, workers assessed their effects of work through selected indicators before and during the COVID-19 pandemic (Etheridge et al., 2020). Changes in productivity before the pandemic period and in May–June 2020 were examined. Workers said they were on average as successful as before the pandemic. However, work performance has been shown to vary significantly across socioeconomic groups, industries, and occupations. Workers in occupations that are less suitable for work from home have lower productivity than before the pandemic. Further, women had lower productivity, as well as workers with lower incomes. In contrast, workers who have attractive occupations and high incomes show greater success. For women, work is also influenced by the family environment. At the time of locking due to isolation and excessive reference to each other, the demands of children from their mothers are especially emphasized, which reduces the available working hours and working capacities of mothers. In addition, women are more likely to work in occupations that are not suitable for working from home.

There are especially big differences between those who worked from home before the pandemic and those who started working from home during the pandemic due to the force of circumstances. While the former often increased productivity in the latter it dropped significantly. However, it should be noted that productivity during a pandemic also depended on a number of factors not most often included in the analysis, such as the type of economic activity in which they operate (tourism is known to be most affected) is the very nature of the activity, which is less compatible with work from home, and numerous specific limitations in each industry.

At the end of this review, it is worth mentioning a study that, among other things, compares the advantages and disadvantages of working from home of scientific and academic staff before and during the COVID-19 pandemic (Aczel et al., 2017). Of the 704 professors and researchers who completed the questionnaire (75% were from the social sciences). Unlike most other professions, as many as 94% of scientists said they worked more during the pandemic than before. However, of this percentage, as many as 47% said that working from home made their work less efficient, 23% felt that they achieved greater efficiency during the lockdown, while 30% did not notice differences compared to the period before the pandemic. The picture is more unfavorable if efficiency is observed in families with children; as many as 58% of scientists from families with children showed less efficiency in working from home during a pandemic, 20% thought they were more efficient, and 20% found no difference.

PSYCHOSOCIAL PROBLEMS DUE WORKING FROM HOME

As we said earlier, research on work from home can be thematically divided into two basic units: those that deal with mostly positive aspects of work from home and those that deal with negative aspects.

The first group was mostly discussed in the first section of this introductory part. Psychosocial issues can also be divided into positive and negative.

The positive:

- Freedom and autonomy
- Motivation
- Self-discipline
- Job satisfaction
- Good sleep
- Enjoying work
- Social support for family, relatives, and friends
- Good social connection with colleagues
- Good mental health
- Good physical health

The negative:

- Social isolation
- Anxiety
- Concerns
- Irritability

- Resentment
- Feelings of guilt
- Frustration
- Stress
- Burnout
- Depression
- Suicidal thoughts
- Obsessive preoccupation with work
- Presentism
- Feeling of social disconnection with colleagues and management, loss of self-confidence and identity
- Loss of boundaries between work and private life
- Psychosomatic disorders
- Disorders of the musculoskeletal system
- Poor social communication with colleagues and employers
- Alienation from family, relatives, and friends
- Alienation from coworkers
- Mental disorders

First about some positive psychosocial aspects. In the previously mentioned study by an Indonesian author (Susilo et al., 2020), working from home significantly contributed to increasing job satisfaction. That is why the author points out that working from home is the best choice to increase job satisfaction. Further, a strong positive association with motivation was found; those who work from home significantly increase their motivation to work. The effect at work, however, is not in a direct positive relationship with working from home, but in an indirect one; only with the growth of satisfaction and motivation can a better performance be expected in those who work from home. A direct positive link has been found between work environment and job satisfaction, which is why the authors recommend to policy makers that if they want to increase job satisfaction, they improve the work environment of employees at home. Contrary to expectations, motivation is not significantly related to job satisfaction. Therefore, they conclude that the usual efforts of companies to increase motivation to work do not contribute to increasing job satisfaction of those who work at home. The author provides an original explanation for this unexpected result; under psychological pressure due to the COVID-19 pandemic home employees "forgot" about motivation, and at the same time are satisfied that they work from home, especially since others do not work from home or have lost their jobs (Susilo et al., 2020).

A good working environment significantly increases work performance, which is in line with previous findings.

It is our assumption that the family environment plays such a role in Indonesian society because of some traditionally religious and collectivist patterns that are especially manifested in the lives of Indonesian families. Therefore, companies in Indonesia are recommended that improving the various parameters of the work environment is a sure way to increase work performance. On the other hand, job satisfaction significantly increases work performance. Motivation at work also increases performance, as a result of which the author of this chapter recommends the management of Indonesian companies that if they want to increase work performance, a good way is to increase motivation. The most important implication of the study is that companies that want to achieve their organizational goals must achieve that employee are satisfied with their work and that they are motivated.

The negative aspects of working from home have their origin in a wide range of psychological and psychosocial problems. It is very important to note that the line between positive and negative aspects is sometimes very thin.

The second study, which represents a meta-analysis of 308 studies, different psychological outcomes of remote work are analyzed (Lewis et al., 2020). New modalities of work contain two important determinants: they are supported by new information and communication technologies and have clearly defined goals (Nijp et al., 2016).

The most significant advantage of new forms of work is that they increase worker autonomy (Steenbergen et al., 2018) and strengthen motivation (Pritchard & Payne, 2003). A sense of control over the schedule of work activities and the impact on establishing a balance between work and private life creates a sense of satisfaction (Beckers et al., 2012) which all results in good mental health (Kotera, Green, & Shefield, 2019).

THE NEGATIVE ASPECTS OF WORKING FROM HOME ORIGINATE FROM PSYCHOLOGICAL AND PSYCHOSOCIAL ISSUES

It is very important to note that the line is sometimes very thin.

Remote employees often lose the support of colleagues (Halford, 2005). The autonomy of remote workers can be significantly reduced due to unrealistic expectations of the help that others can provide in achieving their goals (Mazmanian et al., 2013). Poor mental health of people working remotely is a major problem for most countries (Kestrel, 2019). In Great Britain, 16 million working days were lost in 2016 due to poor mental health, which cost Britain 65 billion pounds or 3% of gross national income. Dutch workers have the most mental health problems in Organization for Economic Cooperation and Development (OECD) countries and cost the Netherlands 3% of national income annually (OECD, 2014). In the European Union, due to depression, the total costs of losses due to falling productivity, treatment costs and disability benefits amount to 620 billion euros (Matrix Insight Economic, 2013).

The situation in Japan is much worse; 66% of Japanese workers stated that their mental health was impaired, and their claims for damages due to these problems have increased nine times in the last two decades (Ministry of Health, Labor and Welfare, Japan, 2019).

After this rather gloomy epidemiological picture in Europe, the authors point out that the support and understanding of the work organization and family are the most important for successful remote working and maintaining mental health (De Bloom et al., 2017). They suggest a number of measures to prevent mental problems, including simple ones such as chat breaks, short morning walks and the like. However, they also point to some strategic moves modelled on Japan such as the four-day work week that led to a 40% increase in productivity in Japan (Jackman, 2020).

Social isolation: Among the negative phenomena, social isolation occupies a significant place. As far back as 1983, in the United Kingdom, as many as 60% of remote workers identified isolation as the biggest problem (Huvs, 1984). Remote workers come to this knowledge by comparing themselves with others; others become a barometer for ourselves (Mann & Holdsworth, 2000; Mann et al., 2000).

According to another researcher, social isolation and loneliness are key to the occurrence of other negative emotional states such as anxiety, nervousness, irritability, anxiety, and the like (Rook, 1984).

Presentism: An issue that managers often unjustifiably value is presentism. Presentism does not only mean extended working hours but also work in a sick state. Presentism is indicated by the appearance of reduced absenteeism and pain. Instead of not doing his job that day due to health problems, he only asks for a free morning, and often the sick person works all day. He should return to work when he is completely recovered, and not take a free morning. At the core of presentism is the fear of a bad impression that work interruptions can leave on employers and the expectation that employers will especially appreciate his motivation to work even when he is ill. This seems to be a problem for all workers, not just those who work remotely. The need for such "proof" is conditioned by the effort to prevent all possible unpleasant events related to the crisis, which is first repercussed by dismissals or shortened work engagements, salary reductions, and so forth.

During the 1990s and the beginning of this century, the lack of technical support was also key to the success of remote working. However, with the development of new technologies, this is a largely overcome problem today.

Slow career advancement: Remote workers complain of slow career advancement because their work is insufficiently visible to employers, while all jobs and social promotions of office workers are valorised when employers make promotion decisions (Haddon & Levis, 1994) They can get the impression that they are bypassed in all important actions and processes of the company (Turner, 1998).

Working from home and gender: Women who work from home are at a disadvantage not only because they have two working hours, but also because performing family roles is not considered work for them. Work is considered to be going to the office (Mann et al., 2000). While working from home is recognized for men, it is not for women, so both of their work from home remains marginalized (Hall, 1972). In contrast, men derive their identity from their professional role and a combination of different forms of work increases their reputation in the social environment. Even if they work from home, women are expected to do family chores because the family is their "natural" environment.

Due to all of the above, women who work from home experience more stress than men who work from home and their physical and mental health is more at risk (Ellison, 1999; Hall, 1972).

The responses of women who work remotely about stressful events are significantly more related to real stresses than those of men who work remotely. If this relevant finding is taken into account, then women who work remotely are more exposed to stressful events and have somewhat poorer mental and physical health (Mann & Holdsworth, 2000). When it comes to reporting subjective pain, no significant differences were found between men and women who work from home (Song & Gao, 2019).

Seven studies examined the impact of gender on the mental health of home workers (Eddleston & Mulki, 2017; Hornung & Glasser, 2009; Kazekami, 2020; Song & Gao, 2019). When it comes to reporting subjective pain, no significant differences were found between men and women who work from home (Song & Gaoo, 2019).

Research before the pandemic showed higher levels of stress in women (Bolger et al., 1989; Duxbury et al., 2018; Fan et al., 2019; Karkoulian et al., 2016; Peeters et al., 2005). Based on the results of a survey conducted in early April 2020, women showed significantly higher levels of stress than men at the time of the COVID-19 pandemic (Flesia et al., 2020). The reasons are related to the lack of partner support (Peeters et al., 2005). At the same time, in addition to full-time work, women work an average of 20 more hours per week than men in housework, childcare and care (LeanIn. org. and Survey Monkey, 2020).

Work from home and office work of men: Men who work remotely reported lower stress levels than office workers. In this study, the authors analyze the effect of remote work on the expression of emotions, stress, and the health status of remote workers and office workers (Mann & Holdsworth, 2000).

Both groups do the same types of jobs. The research consists of two studies: qualitative and quantitative. Qualitative analysis singled out seven emotions: stress, loneliness, enjoyment, irritability, anxiety, resentment, guilt, and frustration.

Stress: Stress is an almost chronic phenomenon and most often occurs due to the fear that the deadlines for the completion of work will not be met. Office workers have similar reasons for stress, and in addition, office workers are exposed to constant stressful situations due to travel, due to feelings of hostility and anger due to traffic jams, fear of being late for work and the like (Montreuil & Lippel, 2003).

Loneliness: Loneliness is one of the most intense feelings of people who work remotely. It occurs as a consequence of the lack of social support, as a result of which insecurity and lack of confidence in one's abilities develop. As a result, remote workers feel lonely and abandoned by others. It is interesting to mention that office workers do not have such feelings at all.

Enjoyment: Enjoyment occurs as a result of heightened self-confidence and pride in completed work or work in progress (Pekrun & Frese, 1992). No significant differences were found between the remote workers and the office workers in terms of expressing this emotion.

Irritability: Irritability occurs due to lack of interruption, loss of control over the situation that arises due to obstruction of others (Pekrun & Frese, 1992). In remote workers, irritability increases because people who obstruct are at a great physical distance. This creates even greater frustration because due to the physical distance, remote workers cannot expect the help of colleagues in resolving a conflict situation. Irritation and frustration turn into anger, which leads to stressful situations. There is another situation that irritates remote workers. It is an intrusion of family members into the workspace because it seems to them to be part of a single-family space, which irritates remote workers and brings them into states of frustration, anger and stress.

Concerns: Concerns arise in remote workers due to a lack of support, especially when it comes to difficult tasks or tasks with a short deadline. Being concerns can turn into panic. Office workers have the same problem when finishing work on time.

Resentment: Resentment most often occurs in remote workers as a result of the inability to be excluded from work and the lack of recognition of any kind due to excessive work, but also due to the feeling of frustration in the realization of favorite family activities.

Guilt: Guilt arises from the inability to strike a balance between business and family responsibilities, leading to internal conflicts of remote workers. Guilt is most often felt for not fulfilling promises and obligations towards children. Feelings of guilt are heightened by the fact that children never forget promises and constantly remind parents of their fulfilment.

Frustration: Frustration occurs in both remote and office workers primarily due to a lack of support, with remote workers more often pointing out a lack of technical support and a lack of support from office colleagues and management.

The results of the qualitative analysis showed that remote workers experienced more negative emotions, especially when it comes to loneliness, irritability, worry, and guilt. Office workers estimated that they were only more exposed to stress than remote workers due to the organization of office services and, in particular, due to transport problems. Because the qualitative analysis is based on the attitudes of the respondents, it is not possible to assess what for example is the connection between the subjective experience of stress and real stressful situations, nor whether there is an objective assessment of the severity of certain negative emotions between remote workers and office workers.

In another study, a good operationalization of basic research concepts was performed in order to avoid a certain arbitrariness resulting from qualitative analysis (Mann & Holdsworth, 2000). The results showed that remote workers show significantly more negative emotions and have poorer mental and physical health than office workers. However, the assumption that women who work remotely have poorer mental and physical health than men has not been confirmed.

Interestingly, although office workers in Study 1 (qualitative analysis) reported experiencing higher levels of stress than remote workers, another study found that remote workers had more symptoms of stress than office workers. It is obvious that it is much more important to consider whether there are objectively symptoms of stress than the subjective experience that we are under stress, which was not taken into account enough.

In the final part of the study, the authors recommend a whole repertoire of measures to repair negative emotions and improve physical and mental functioning, which focus on various support measures to be implemented by company managers, various support measures expected from close associates to a range of entertainment and recreational activities that remote workers need to undertake (Mann & Holdsworth, 2000).

Between the declarative acceptance by employers that synchronized measures are necessary to protect endangered mental health and the real situation, we get the impression that there is a rather deep gap. Companies point out that remote work has many benefits for employees that have been talked about a lot before. However, the truth seems to be more on the other side according to which remote working results in higher productivity. The collision between a somewhat idealized image that companies try to place and the real situation can be seen in the extent to which they are committed to the practical implementation of measures to protect the mental and physical health of remote workers; at the end of the last century, of all companies in the U.K. that introduced remote work, less than half had taken any steps to protect the mental and physical health of remote workers.

Depression: Despite all the positive aspects that have been discussed, working from home can cause a number of psychological problems, the most important of which are social isolation, stress, pressure (Holmes et al., 2020) and depression. The author presents an exhaustive symptomatology of depression, which often occurs as a result of a series of psychological symptoms, and we will list it in its entirety. Anxiety, stress and loneliness lead to depression which manifests itself:

- "angry outbursts, irritability and frustration (even because of small things);
- loss of interest and satisfaction in activities such as sex and hobbies;
- sleep disorders, including insomnia and too much sleep;
- fatigue and lack of energy; even small tasks require extra effort;
- increased desire for food;
- anxiety, agitation and restlessness;
- problems with thinking, concentrating, making decisions and remembering things;
- unexplained physical problems, such as back pain or headaches." (Holmes et al., 2020)

The author recommends the following set of behavioral measures to reduce mental and physical symptoms: create a routine, upgrade the apartment, go out in the garden, establish virtual contacts with others, start saying "no" (Holmes et al., 2020).

Burnout: The most common and severe consequence of conflict and imbalance between family and work is burnout (Langballe et al., 2011; Lingard & Francis, 2006; Proost et al., 2004). At the same time, it leaves negative consequences on our psychosocial status (Fiksenbaumet al., 2010; Maslach et al., 2001; Salanova & Lorens, 2008). It previously appeared in the narrow circle of professions (Dyrbye et al., 2011; Keeton et al., 2007) and today it often occurs between different and distant professions (Peeters et al., 2003). Burnout can be defined as "a symptom of personal exhaustion, depersonalization, and reduced personal success" (Maslach, 1982).

In all theories, insufficient resources or excessive work demands are underlined in the occurrence of negative work-house interactions and burnout (Bakker & Demerouti, 1982; Hobfol, 2001; Johnson & Hall, 1988). Most research starts from the assumption that conflict between work and home is key to the onset of burnout (Lingard & Francis, 2006; Dyrbye et al., 2011; Peeters et al., 2005). Some researchers, on the other hand, believe that burnout is mediated between stress and conflicts between work and life. However, the conflict of multiple roles stimulates remote employees to develop new values and skills and apply them in another domain. Thus, they can also play a positive role and at least somewhat prevent combustion. Different combinations of interactions are possible that are associated with better mental and physical health (Grzywacz, 2000; Grzywacz & Bass, 2003).

It is usually assumed that the interactions are work-family with a negative sign. A significant innovation in this study is that the authors also take into account positive interactions (Merecz & Andysz, 2014) which, except in a very small number of studies (Peeters et al., 2005), were overlooked. In addition, the authors took into account both combinations of interactions (work-house and house-work) in a positive and negative direction.

The main finding is that the clusters were dominated by mostly positive interactions—55%.

Only 16% experienced negative interactions, while 29% had no interactions.

The results of this study call into question the theory of segmentation and the necessity of establishing firm boundaries between work and home. Instead of establishing firm boundaries, it is preferable to talk about the continuum of integration—segmentation (Hall & Richter, 1988; Rothbard et al., 2005) and the necessity of overflow when there is a danger of conflict between work and family (Cho et al., 2013).

When it comes to gender relations, no significant differences were found. However, negative interactions were more common in people who worked longer than 10 hours a day. The length of the work is obviously related to burnout (Barnettet al., 1999; Keene & Quadagno, 2004).

The results of the study convincingly showed that segmentation is not a good strategy for overcoming conflicts between work and family in remote workers.

- Psychological and psychosocial problems of special categories of teleworkers

Rotational remote workers have particularly pronounced psychological and psychosocial problems. They mostly work in maritime, mining (oil and gas), construction and energy. In this study, the authors included fourteen countries (from European, to African, Asian, American, and Australian). The interviews were preceded by a meta-analysis of a large number of studies on the negative and positive psychological and psychosocial aspects of the work of rotating remote workers (Lewis et al., 2020.). Given the nature of the work, the sample was predominantly male (81% men and 16% women).

Most workers expressed satisfaction with the conditions provided by the companies they work for: 95% said that for their companies their health came first, 79% said their company was committed to embracing diversity and inclusion, and 78% said they were open to members of all cultures. Workforces are also positively rated in high percentages: 87% are satisfied with work, 88% with accommodation, 78% are satisfied with internet connections, and 69% with leisure content. Most felt they had psychological support. However, 23% thought it was missing. The issue of flexibility was rated the worst because 40% felt that they did not have adequate flexibility in their roles.

In general, rotating workers from Asia, the Middle East, and North Africa were significantly more satisfied with the conditions and organization than those from America and Pacific Asia. Those with longer tenure and leadership positions were also generally more satisfied. Despite all the above positive assessments, 52% of workers pointed out that they become moody and have mental problems while on rotation. Negative and positive consequences of rotational work were classified by researchers into four groups: emotional outcomes, family, social and work outcomes, psychosocial and psychosomatic outcomes, and work-related and organizational outcomes.

When it comes to negative emotional consequences, burnout, loneliness, depression, and suicidal thoughts stand out. By the way, suicidal thoughts are most pronounced in rotary workers at a distance because they are often months thousands of kilometers away from the nearest and in very depressing working conditions, for example, work on offshore oil platforms. The positives include job satisfaction, opportunities for fun and experiences of various excitements.

The negative family factors include concern for the emotional and similar needs of children, problems of adjustment to special conditions and problems of behavior in such conditions, conflicts between business and family obligations, financial pressures to be the sole breadwinner of the family, bad relationships.

The positive family and social factors relate to social ties and the good functioning of the family.

The negative psychosocial and psychosomatic factors most often refer to fatigue and insomnia, stomach problems, and positive—satisfactory length of sleep.

The negative outcomes associated with the company are the intention to give up further work, the feeling of lack of competence and motivation, while the positive are the enjoyment of work and the feeling of belonging and togetherness, as well as good friendships.

In the final part of the study, the authors present a number of recommendations, among which are particularly important those related to raising the safety culture of companies to a higher level, especially strategies to preserve the mental health of rotating workers and increase flexibility.

- Effects of work from home on physical health

Searching the database of 1,557 papers, published from 2007 to 2020, on the health effects of working from home on mental and physical health of employees, the authors in the next study with strict methodological criteria singled out 21 studies for further analysis (Oakman et al., 2020)

The effects of working from home on physical health: Researchers in other studies have reported physical health problems on the basis of subjective assessments (pain, problems in the musculoskeletal system, etc.) (Fílardí et al., 2020; Gimenez-Nadal et al., 2020). Civil servants working from home generally pointed out that they had no physical health problems (Fílardí et al., 2020). Another group from a financial company working from home reported a decline in physical fitness, which did not have negative consequences on their employment status (Nijp et al., 2016).

The effects of working from home on mental health: There are significantly more studies in which researchers have addressed mental health. These include the following outcomes: well-being, stress, depression, fatigue, quality of life, stress, and happiness. Researchers in nine studies address the environmental, physical, and psychosocial impacts on the mental health of those who work from home (Anderson et al., 2015; Bentley et al., 2016; Eddleston & Mulki, 2017, Golden, 2012, Grant et al., 2013; Major, et al., 2008; Sardeshmukh et al., 2012; Suh & Lee, 2017; Vander et al., 2017). The authors point out that working from home can have positive or negative effects on mental health depending on the behavior of family members, organizational factors in the company, social ties, especially outside working hours, and so forth (Bentley et al., 2016; Grant et al., 2013; Sardeshmukh et al., 2012; Suh & Lee, 2017; Vander et al., 2017).

Positive or negative effects are not unambiguous; they are the result of complex constellations of factors. Less time pressures to get work done at home, giving more autonomy to employees working from home, and a better work-life balance without conflict will certainly result in less exhaustion, less stress, and better mental health. We have repeatedly pointed out that working overtime affects the occurrence of mental disorders. However, if it is not a question of work exaggerations for a longer period of time, extended time will not lead to mental health disorders if the worker has the support of colleagues and superiors. Another study, however, showed that the length of work from home affects the occurrence of depressive symptoms. Workers from home have been shown to have fewer depressive symptoms than office workers if they have not worked for more than eight hours (Henke et al., 2016).

Men who worked full time from home exhibited higher levels of stress than office workers (Kazekami, 2020).

When it comes to reporting subjective pain, no significant differences were found between men and women who work from home (Song & Gao, 2019).

Shortened working hours for employees working from home have led to an increase in autonomy and quality of life. However, this relationship was significant only for men, but not for women (Eddelston & Mulkey, 2017). Men who work from home show an increased level of stress, but also happiness, while women have not shown that. No significant differences in mental health were found between women working from home and in the office.

In the discussion, the authors propose measures to improve the mental and physical health of people working from home that can be summarized in five groups: organizational measures, support of associates, technical support, support for border management, addressing gender inequalities.

Due to significantly different working conditions caused by the pandemic in the domain of organizational measures, the authors advocate regular communication in which work tasks, roles and mutual expectations are precisely and clearly defined. Human resource support is needed (Hayman, 2010; Kaduk et al., 2019) and financial assistance for special expenses due to work from home (Major et al., 2008).

Collaboration of coworkers involves supporting all forms of formal and informal communication via the internet and social contacts that can replace office day (Bentley et al., 2016, Golden, 2012, Song & Gao, 2019).

Technical support requires the application of the latest technologies in work from home and appropriate training (Bosua et al., 2013; Fílardí et al., 2020).

It is necessary to establish boundaries between work, family and recreational activities. The most efficient way is to educate both employees from home and managers (Eddelson & Mulki, 2017).

Instead of a narrowed vision of the need to reduce gender inequalities, the authors offer a broader and more acceptable strategy that would include the development of preventive measures to preserve mental health that would be adapted to members of both gender and all ages (Daverth et al., 2016; Kossek & Lautsch, 2018).

Stress and burnout is a consequence of working from home during the COVID-19 pandemic. The latest research, which we will present in this literature review, is about the connection between the occurrence of stress and burnout at work due to the COVID-19 pandemic. A few papers have been written on this topic on large samples (Center for Disease Control and Prevention, 2020; Petterson et al,, 2020). At the same time, thinking about when the economy will restart due to the pandemic, it was considered that working from home would be a permanent option (Lavelle, 2020). As early as April 2020, 3.9 billion people were locked up, and in the U.S. 90% (Secon & Woodward, 2020) and more than 50% of the world's population (Sandford, 2020). With the extension of the lock, there was more and more talk about worrying phenomena with mental health: increasing stress, with increased anxiety and depression (Center for National Health Statistics, 2020) and with increasing self-harm and suicide based on comparisons with previous major job losses (Petterson et al,, 2020). Not enough attention is paid to the mental health of those who have never worked remotely due to a pandemic, nor to those who have had little experience with that type of work.

The COVID-19 pandemic has led to a large increase in work from home, which has led to stress for many who started working from home for the first time (Rigotti et al., 2020). Chronic stress, which inevitably leads to burnout, occurs in a number of occupations, especially helping ones (Gray & Muramatsy, 2011; Maslah & Leiter, 2016; Shirom et al., 2016; Wood et al., 2020). In other studies, the source of stress is seen due to role overload due to balancing work and family roles (Bolger et al., 1989; Duxbury et al., 2018), lack of experience of organizational support (Stamper & Johlke, 2003) and adverse impact of physical environment on work ability (Vischer, 2007). Each of these studies and all together support the theory that stress is a consequence of roles overload (Duxbury et al., 2018) resulting in a "spillover" of roles from family to work and from work to family (Bolger et al., 1989). "The spillover" generates or deepens conflicts in the family (Fan et al., 2019; Lim & Kim, 2014;).

Psychological burnout syndrome occurs as a result of long-term special mental and physical exhaustion caused by stressful social situations. Symptomatology is characterized by a feeling of isolation, abandonment, cynicism, reduced efficiency. Burnout can significantly reduce productivity and job satisfaction (Kristensen et al., 2016; Maslach & Leiter, 2005).

More important results of the study are that men who worked full time during the pandemic and those who worked before the lockout had higher perceived levels of stress and burnout at work than before the pandemic.

Although stress levels increased on average for all participants, they increased significantly more for workers who did not have flexible working hours before the pandemic and for women. However, no differences were found between full-time and part-time workers.

The results support the theoretical understanding that stress is a consequence of "spillover" and "burdening with roles" that take place in the same environment (Bolger et al., 1989; Duxbury, Stevenson, and Higgins, 2018) especially for women (Fan, Lam, and Moen, 2019; Flesia et al., 2020; LeanIn.org. and Survey Monkey, 2020).

THE METHOD

For the empirical analysis of the set goals, we constructed three questionnaires (appendices at the end of the chapter)

The first refers to the psychosocial adjustment to new forms of work. The second examines the influence of economic factors on new forms of work. The third treats the advantages and disadvantages of freelancing.

Each of the questionnaires (appendices at the end of the chapter) covers all important aspects related to the basic content of the questionnaire.

The questionnaire construction procedure was relatively complex and lengthy. We first produced a large number of statements for each type of questionnaire (approximately the initial versions were five times more extensive than the final version). Professor Mirjana Radović-Marković certainly has the greatest credit for the second and third questionnaire, who knows the research problem best and who therefore performed triage of questions relatively easily in order to achieve satisfactory validity and reliability. Her initial assessment proved to be largely accurate. We supplemented the validation of the finally accepted claims in each questionnaire with assessments by three independent experts for each area. In the final version, only the statements that all three independent experts assessed as satisfactory remained.

THE SAMPLE

The sample consists of 1,031 respondents from four countries of the Western Balkans: 201 from BiH, 201 from Montenegro, 221 from Northern Macedonia, and 408 from Serbia. The sample has a suitable character because the "sample" includes everyone who works from home and who has agreed to fill in the questionnaire in electronic form. Due to the lack of representativeness, all generalizations of results to the general population of those who work from home are unreliable and may serve more as some major landmarks in future research.

With very scarce personal financial resources, it was not possible to achieve a more acceptable representativeness (see Table 4.1).

Table 4.1

How They Work Primarily From Home

How do you primarily work from home?	Bosnia and Herzegovina	Montenegro	Northern Macedonia	Serbia	Total
Any other form of work from home	72	152	90	204	518
	35.8%	77.2%	40.7%	55.1%	52.4%
I work as a "freelancer" (in the "Gig" Economy, without a contract with the employer, continuously or on projects using on-line platforms	129	45	131	166	471
	64.2%	22.8%	59.3%	44.9%	47.6%
Total	201	197	221	370	989
	100.0%	100.0%	100.0%	100.0%	100.0%

Table 4.2 shows that almost half are freelancers (47.6%). That percentage is almost three times higher in BiH than in Montenegro, while Northern Macedonia is significantly approaching it. It is important to emphasize that this is a consequence of the appropriate coverage of the electronic survey and is by no means representative.

KEY FINDINGS

We presented the distribution of items from the Scale of Psychosocial Adjustment by reducing the 5-point scale to a three-point scale in order to more clearly notice the significant numerical differences between the four countries (see Table 4.2).

It is important to recall that the negative claims on this scale recoded.

From Table 4.1 it can be seen that for the first claim "Since I started my own business, I have a lot less time for myself and my hobbies" there are significant differences among the states. We applied *ANOVA* ($F = 9,881$; $p = 0.000$). The respondents from Montenegro actually have much less time for their hobbies and activities than respondents from Bosnia and

Table 4.2

Distribution of items From the Psychosocial Adjustment Scale in the Four Countries of the Western Balkans

Statements**	Bosnia and Herzegovina			Montenegro			Northern Macedonia			Serbia			Total:		
	No	Indecis.	Yes	No	Indecis.	Yes	No	Indecis.	Yes	No	Indecisive	Yes	No	Indecis.	Yes
1.	19.4	37.8	42.8	64.3	27.4	28.4	37.1	9.5	53.4	34.3	17.2	48.6			
2.	15.5	20.4	64.2	17.9	27.9	54.3	19.0	11.8	69.3	23.3	13.5	63.2			
3.	15.0	18.9	65.1	25.3	22.4	52.3	14.9	15.4	69.7	16.2	11.8	72.1	17.5	16.0	66.6
4.	9.5	15.9	74.7	24.9	23.4	51.6	20.4	11.8	67.9	16.9	17.2	65.4	17.8	17.0	65.3
5.	15.5	31.8	52.8	17.4	30.3	52.3	22.6	24.0	53.4	26.0	24.5	49.5	21.5	27.0	51.5
6.	7.5	17.9	74.6	3.5	29.4	67.2	20.8	13.1	66.1	9.0	18.4	72.5	10.2	19.3	70.5
7.	14.9	25.4	59.7	11.0	30.3	58.7	17.2	17.1	65.6	16.7	22.3	60.1	15.3	23.4	61.2
8.	10.0	28.4	61.7	9.5	24.9	65.7	22.2	19.0	58.9	16.4	26.5	57.2	15.0	24.9	60.1
9.	20.9	25.4	53.7	33.8	28.9	37.3	23.1	19.9	57.1	16.4	20.8	62.7	22.1	23.1	54.8
10.	38.3	27.4	34.3	54.7	18.4	26.8	40.8	27.1	32.2	33.8	28.4	37.8	40.2	26.0	33.8
11.	10.0	20.9	69.2	21.9	28.4	49.8	17.2	17.6	65.2	12.3	14.5	73.3	14.7	19.1	66.1
12.	3.5	14.4	82.1	4.0	21.9	74.1	17.6	13.6	68.8	5.9	11.8	82.4	7.15	14.6	77.8
13.	9.5	20.4	70.2	14.5	18.4	67.2	21.2	15.8	62.9	9.6	13.5	77.0	13.0	16.3	70.7

* The numbers are given in percentages

** 1. Since I started my own business, I have a lot less time for myself and my hobbies

2. Working from home does not prevent me from devoting enough time and motivation to engage in physical activities (exercise/sports)

3. Working from home has negatively affected the amount and quality of sleep.

(Table contained on next page)

4. Since I work from home, I pay less attention to my family or partner.

5. Since I work from home, I have more time to hang out with friends.

6. The job I am currently running fulfils me.

7. The current income I earn is enough to cover all my basic needs

8. I am confident in the future success of the business I am currently running

9. I have trouble separating my job from my private life

10. I would like to have more contact with other people during my work

11. Since I work from home, I feel more tense and upset

12. My family and close friends mostly support me in my current job.

13. During work from home, others (family, friends, neighbors) do not disturb me and I can fully dedicate myself to work.

94

Herzegovina ($I\!-\!J$ = $-$ 0.62189; p = 0.000), the respondents from Northern Macedonia ($I\!-\!J$ = $-$0.61165; p = 0.000) and the respondents from Serbia ($I\!-\!J$ = $-$0.58224; p = 0.000).

To the second statement "Working from home does not prevent me from devoting enough time and motivation to engage in physical activities (exercise/sports)" the respondents from Montenegro gave negative answers significantly more often than the respondents from Northern Macedonia ($I\!-\!J$ = $-$0.3224; p = 0.012) and from Serbia less than from Northern Macedonia ($I\!-\!J$ = $-$0.2159; p = 0.049) although this difference is almost on the verge of significance). According to this claim, no statistically significant differences were found between Serbia and Montenegro. It can be concluded that respondents from Montenegro have had more problems and less motivation to engage in physical activities than those from Northern Macedonia since working from home, while in this respect they do not differ significantly from those from Serbia and BiH.

Table 4.1 shows that the respondents from Montenegro were relatively more faced with reduced and poor-quality sleep due to work from home; almost a quarter (22.4%) said they had trouble sleeping. This was confirmed by the findings of $ANOVA$ (F = 10.038; p = 0.000). The respondents from Montenegro had significantly more sleep problems due to work from home than those in BiH ($I\!-\!J$ = $-$0.35821; p = 0.004) than those from Northern Macedonia ($I\!-\!J$ = $-$0.52509; p = 0.000) and those from Serbia ($I\!-\!J$ = $-$0.56940; p = 0.000, Table 4.1).

When asked: "Since I work from home, I pay less attention to my family or partner," the respondents from Montenegro again pointed out in a quarter of cases that they pay less attention to family or partner because of working from home (Table 4.1). These differences were confirmed using $ANOVA$ (F = 8.243; p = 0.000). The respondents from Montenegro have been paying less attention to family and partners since working from home than the respondents from Bosnia and Herzegovina ($I\!-\!J$ = $-$0.60697; p = 0.000) of Northern Macedonia ($I\!-\!J$ = $-$0.35814) and Serbia ($I\!-\!J$ = $-$0.43638).

According to the fifth statement "Since I work from home, I have more time to hang out with friends," no statistically significant differences were found between countries (F = 1.182; p = 0.316). Table 4.1 shows that the lack of time to hang out with friends due to work from home is pronounced in even more than half of the cases, and more than a quarter cannot estimate that accurately. However, it is noticed that the percentage of those who do not think that they have less time for friends because of work from home is higher in Northern Macedonia, and especially in Serbia, while that percentage is the lowest in BiH, followed by Montenegro. However, these differences do not reach the degree of statistical significance and should be viewed as mild tendencies.

The sixth statement "The job I am currently running fulfils me" shows that respondents are generally satisfied with the work they do from home. The percentage of dissatisfied people ranges from 3.5% (Montenegro) to 9% (Serbia, see Table 4.1). The only exceptions are respondents from Northern Macedonia, where the percentage of dissatisfied with work from home reaches as much as 20.8% (Table 4.1). The *ANOVA* also showed that the respondents from Northern Macedonia were significantly less satisfied with their current work from home than all the other (F = 4.542; p = 0.004). They are less satisfied than the respondents from BiH (I–J = –0.2982; p = 0.005), Montenegro (I–J = –0.2683; p = 0.012) and Serbia (I–J = –0.3220; p = 0.000).

Three-fifths of the respondents from all four countries are very satisfied or satisfied with current income, while the percentage of those who are dissatisfied is only about one-sixth (Table 4.1). Similar to the work that the respondents do from home that they are most satisfied with, the respondents are also satisfied with their current income, although to a lesser extent (see Table 4.1). However, differences between countries in terms of current income do not reach the level of statistical significance (F = 0.122; p = 0.947).

The respondents in all four countries are in about three-fifths of cases confident in the future success of the work they are currently doing (Table 4.1). No statistically significant differences were found between the countries using *ANOVA* (F = 2.463; p = 0.061). However, it should be noted that the respondents from Northern Macedonia are relatively most sceptical about the future success of the work they are currently doing, which may explain that the value of the F test in this case approaches the significance limit of 0.05.

The respondents from Montenegro have more problems than the others to separate their work from home from private life; one-third said they had problems, and much less in other states (see Table 4.1). These relative differences are the largest when it comes to Serbia, where twice as few respondents had these problems (Table 4.1). The differences are statistically significant (F = 14.023; p = 0.000. In relation to BiH, they amount to (I–J = –0.48259; p =0 .000) Northern Macedonia (I–J = –0.46386; p = 0.000) and Serbia (I–J = –0.73101; p = 0.000).

The respondents from Montenegro, less than from the other three countries, want to have contacts with other people while working from home; it should be noted that more than half did not express this wish (Table 4.1). The differences are statistically significant compared to the other three countries; in relation to BiH (I–J = –0.35821; p = 0.000) Northern Macedonia (I–J = – 0.32516; p = 0.015) and Serbia (I–J = –0.50578; p = 0.000).

Due to working from home, the respondents from Montenegro are the most tense and upset (Table 4.1). It is interesting to note that the majority of respondents from BiH said that they do not feel tense and anxious during work from home (about 70%) and similarly those from Northern Macedonia, while the respondents from Serbia in almost three quarters of cases expressed confusion and ambivalence feelings about working at home. The differences are statistically significant when it comes to Montenegro and others, as well as between Serbia and Macedonia ($F = 12.672$; $p = 0.000$). Respondents from Montenegro are significantly more tense and anxious during work from home than those from BiH ($I–J = –0.50746$; $p = 0.000$) of Northern Macedonia ($I–J = 0.36402$; $p = 0.000$) and Serbia ($I–J = –0.62533$; $p = 0.000$). Respondents from Serbia were less tense and anxious than respondents from Northern Macedonia ($I–J = 0.26131$; $p = 0.009$).

Relatives and friends of the respondents supported them in their work from home in very similar percentages, while they were relatively least supported by relatives and friends in Northern Macedonia, followed by Montenegro (see Table 4.1). The respondents from BiH were significantly more supportive of working from home than the respondents in Northern Macedonia and Montenegro, as well as the respondents from Serbia compared to Macedonia and Montenegro ($F = 10.718$; $p = 0.000$). Relatives and friends are significantly more supportive in BiH than in Northern Macedonia ($I–J = 0.4053$; $p = 0.000$) and Montenegro ($I–J = 0.2189$; $p = 0.033$). In Serbia, they also support more than in Northern Macedonia ($I–J = 0.4495$; $p = 0.000$) and Montenegro ($I–J = 0.2631$; $p = 0.003$).

BiH and Serbia do not differ significantly from each other.

Finally, family and friends do not interfere with work from home of our respondents and allow them to devote themselves to work in large percentages ranging from just over two-fifths (Northern Macedonia) to over three-quarters (Serbia, see Table 4.1). In that respect, Serbia and BiH are the most similar. However, the differences are still statistically significant ($F = 7,138$; $p = 0,000$). Family, friends, and neighbors are less likely to hinder respondents from Serbia to fully dedicate themselves to work from home than the respondents from Northern Macedonia ($I–J = 0.4342$; $p = 0.000$) and from Montenegro ($I–J = 0.3029$; $p = 0.003$). The respondents from BiH are also less disturbed than those from Macedonia ($I–J = 0.025$, $p = 0.025$). No statistically significant differences were found between Serbia and BiH.

Analysis of the Scale of Psychosocial Adaptation to Work From Home for the Total Sample

We were particularly interested in whether the 13 items on the scale are structured in such a way as to represent special dimensions of the psychosocial consequences of respondents who work from home. To that end, we subjected 13 items to factorization. We applied exploratory factor analysis with varimax rotation. We did not include one item from the scale in the analysis because the answers to it were given in binary form. The scale was recoded from the original form so that all items were unambiguously "in one direction." In this case, the questions that show the negative aspects of working from home are recoded so that their minimum number is 1 and their maximum is 5.

Crombach's Alpha is at a good level when the scale is processed in this way and amounts to 0.849 (Table 4.3).

Table 4.3

KMO I Bartlett's Test Adequacy 0.884

Kaiser-Meyer-Olkin Measure of Sampling Adequacy		0.884
Bartlett's Test of Sphericity	Approx. Chi-Square	3,286.374
	df	78
	Sig.	0.000

All communalities are generally high. Only the answers to the question about engaging in sports and physical activities have the lowest saturations. This is probably due to the simple fact that a solid percentage of people are not physically active at all. That is why they cannot answer anything too meaningful.

The indicators performed so far point to a unique conclusion that the scale has good metric properties.

Two factors have been singled out that together explain 44.508 of the variances. The Scree Plot (Figure 4.1) indicates one dominant factor. By interpreting the distribution of items in the two-factor model, a generally meaningful structure was obtained.

Differences In Sociodemographic Characteristics and Factor Scores of the Respondents in Four Countries

Let us recall the important remarks from the beginning of this chapter that our sample is apposite and therefore it is difficult to claim representativeness of research results. As we mentioned, this was conditioned by limited research opportunities at the time of COVID-19, and in part by very limited financial resources.

Figure 4.1

The Scree Plot Scales of Psychosocial Adjustment

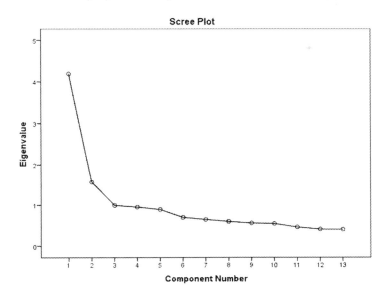

Table 4.4

Matrix of Rotated Components

	Component	
	1	**2**
Since I work from home, I feel more tense and upset	.728	.276
I have trouble separating my job from my private life	.726	.113
Working from home has negatively affected the amount and quality of sleep.	.723	,222
Since I work from home, I pay less attention to my family or partner.	.708	.265
Since I started my own business, I have a lot less time for myself and my hobbies	.616	.157
I would like to have more contact with other people during my work	,483	–.008
I am confident in the stability and future success of the work I am currently doing	.011	.764
The current income I earn is enough to cover all my basic needs.	–.042	.750
The job I am currently doing fulfils me.	.206	.656
My family and close friends mostly support me in my current job.	.290	.586

(Table continued on next page)

Table 4.4 (Continued)

Matrix of Rotated Components

	Component	
	1	2
During work from home, others (family, friends, neighbors) do not disturb me and I can fully dedicate myself to work.	.256	.498
Since I work from home, I have more time to hang out with friends.	.274	.452
Working from home does not prevent me from devoting enough time and motivation to engage in physical activities (exercise/sports).	.120	.418

Conventionally, we singled out those above 0.400 as significant saturations.

A clean, easily interpretable structure was obtained.

The first, strongest factor explains 32.220 of the variance.

The following items stood out on it:

• Since I work from home, I feel more tense and upset.	0.728
• I have problems separating my work from private life.	0.726
• Working from home has negatively affected the amount and quality of sleep.	0.723
• Since I work from home I pay less attention to family or ground floor.	0.708
• I have a lot less time since I started my own business for myself and for my hobbies.	0.616
• I would like to have more contact during the work with other people.	0.483

Recall that negative statements are recoded

We called this first factor the factor of protective effects of work from home on physical and mental health.

The second factor explains 12.288 of the variance. In it with saturations above 0.400 the following items singled out:

• I am confident in the stability and future success of the job I am currently doing.	0.764
• The current income I earn is enough to cover all my basic needs.	0.750
• The job I am currently doing fulfils me.	0.656
• My family and close friends mostly support me in my current job.	0.586
• During work from home, others (family, friends, neighbors) do not disturb me and I can fully dedicate myself to work.	0.498
• Since I work from home, I have more time to socialize with my friends.	0.452
• Working from home does not prevent me from devoting enough time and motivation to engage in physical activity (exercise/sports).	0.418

(Table continued on next page)

Table 4.4 (Continued)

Matrix of Rotated Components

We called the second factor the factor of satisfying professional aspirations and satisfying needs.

We were particularly interested in whether there were statistically significant differences in the factors between countries. To that end, we did *ANOVA* by factor scores. Significance of differences in both factors was determined; according to the first factor, it is more significant (F = 22.924; p = 0.000). According to the second factor F = 2.905; p = 0.034.

According to the first factor, the respondents from Montenegro due to working from home are significantly less exposed stress effects on mental and physical health than the respondents from BiH ($I–J$ = –0.55725326; p = 0.000) Northern Macedonia ($I–J$ = –0.52736686; p = 0.000) and Serbia ($I–J$ = –0.68283202);

According to the second factor, the respondents from Northern Macedonia are significantly less satisfied with work from home and the realization of needs arising from such work than the respondents from Montenegro ($I–J$ = –0.25974146; p = 0.008) and Bosnia and Herzegovina ($I–J$ = –0.23027956; p = 0.018) while it does not differ significantly from Serbia

Gender: There were 547 male and 484 female respondents in the sample. There were no statistically significant differences by gender by country, nor by factor scores.

Age: Using *ANOVA*, statistically significant differences were found by age (F = 56.938; p = 0.000). The respondents in Serbia are older than everyone else; from BiH ($I–J$ = 11.24693; p = 0.000), Montenegro ($I–J$ = 4.85389; p = 0.000) and Northern Macedonia ($I–J$ = 1.94155; p = 0.004). The respondents of Northern Macedonia are older than those from BiH ($I–J$ = 9.30537; p = 0.000) and Montenegro ($I–J$ = 2.91234; p = 0.004). The respondents from Montenegro are older than respondents from BiH ($I–J$ = 6.39303; p = 0.000).

We can conclude that in our apposite sample, the oldest respondents are from Serbia, followed by Northern Macedonia and Montenegro, and the youngest from BiH.

We examined the correlation between age and factor scores using the Pearson correlation coefficient. A slight negative correlation was found between age and factor score on the second factor (r = –0.66; p = 0.033). So, the elderly are less satisfied with the job, salary, and support provided by family, relatives, friends, and neighbors.

Using the $X2$ test, statistically significant differences were found among those working from home in four states. In BiH, there are significantly more of those with secondary education, and in Montenegro with higher and tertiary education ($X2$ = 77.820; df = 9; p = 0,000). It should not be lost sight of that this result may have been influenced by appropriate, selective sample selection.

ACTIVITIES FROM HOME BY COUNTRIES

Table 4.5

Activities From Home by Country

Activities	Bosnia and Herzegovina		Montenegro		Northern Macedonia		Serbia		Total	
	N	%	N	%	N	%	N	%	N	%
Administration	1	0.5	1	0.5	0	0.0	0	0.0	2	0.2
Other	30	14.9	13	6.5	8	3.6	16	3.9	67	6.5
Economics, law, finance, research	8	4.0	5	2.5	3	1.4	21	5.1	37	3.6
Construction	5	2.5	13	6.5	12	5.4	23	5.6	53	5.1
Industry	17	8.5	15	7.5	23	10.4	39	9.6	94	9.1
IT and programming	52	25.9	4	2.0	22	10.0	30	7.4	108	10.5
Cosmetic and hairdressing services	6	3.0	8	4.0	3	1.4	16	3.9	33	3.2
Marketing	9	4.5	2	1.0	5	2.3	14	3.4	30	2.9
Education	22	10.9	39	19.4	51	23.1	65	15.9	177	17.2
Traffic	1	0.5	18	9.0	12	5.4	8	2.0	39	3.8
Trade	35	17.4	58	28.9	53	24.0	124	30.4	270	26.2
Tourism	11	5.5	23	11.4	23	0.4	39	9.6	96	9.3
Art (web design	4	2.0	2	1.0	6	2.7	13	3.2	25	2.4
Total	201	100.0	201	100.0	221	100.0	408	100.0	1031	100.0

Using Spearman's correlation coefficient, a negative correlation was found between the first factor and the level of education ($R = -0.138$; $p = 0.000$). The more educated are less exposed to mental and health problems due to work from home.

Length of working from home: According to the length of working from home, the respondents from BiH work the shortest on average, and from Montenegro the longest from home, followed by Serbia from Serbia ($X2 = 39.400$; $df = 3$; $p = 0.000$).

A negative correlation was found between the length of working from home with the first factor ($Ro = -0.121$; $p = 0.002$) but also with the second factor ($Ro = 0.097$; $p = 0.002$). Those who work longer from home feel less mental and physical tension) than those who work shorter, but also have less satisfaction of professional and other needs.

The subsequent analysis of freelancing will show that our conclusion about the good psychosocial adaptability of respondents who work from home is not excessive. Despite the fact that freelancers are an elite part of the population working from home and at a distance and the coryphaeus of the digital age, the mentioned four countries of the Western Balkans have made their work significantly more difficult due to lack of legal regulations or restrictive measures in the field of health and pension insurance. In that respect, the worst situation is in Serbia. Despite that, freelancing in Serbia is very developed; according to the number of freelancers in relation to the number of inhabitants, Serbia is on the tenth place in the world. This leads to the unequivocal conclusion that freelancers in Serbia (and for the most part in the Western Balkans) are a very resilient work category. Similar conclusions could be applied to some Southeast Asian countries, such as to Pakistan where new forms of teleworking are extremely developed. However, unlike Serbia, freelancers in Pakistan enjoy various types of state aid and support.

Taking into account the way of working from home in four countries, it turned out that freelancers are significantly less represented in Montenegro, and significantly more represented in BiH ($X2 = 83.746$; $df = 3$; $p = 0.000$). This result should, however, be taken with caution, taking into account the method of sampling (Table 4.6).

Using the $X2$ test, statistically significant differences were found ($X2 = 83.746$; $df = 3$; $p = 0.000$). There are significantly fewer freelancers in

Table 4.6

Ways of Working From Home in BiH. Montenegro. Northern Macedonia. and Serbia

Way of working from home	BiH		Montenegro		Northern Macedonia		Serbia		Total	
"Freelancer" (in the "Gig Economy" without a contract with the employer, continuously or by projects using online	129	64.2	45	22.8	131	59.3	166	44.9	471	47.6
Any other way of working from home	72	35.8	152	77.2	90	40.7	204	55.1	518	52.4
Total	201	100.0	197	100.0	221	100.0	370	100.0	989	100.0

Montenegro, and significantly more in BiH. It is important to note that these differences do not have to be a reflection of the actual situation, but of the previously mentioned method of sample selection. However, according to unofficial information, freelancing is the least developed in Montenegro, so these differences do not have to be accidental.

Psychosocial Adjustment Scale and Economic Aspects of Working From Home

In this part, we will analyze the impact of psychosocial adjustment on the economic aspects of working from home, that is, which economic aspects of working from home the respondents are best and to which the worst adjusted in psychosocial terms. Before that, we will examine whether there are statistically significant differences in certain economic aspects of working from home between countries.

The first question is "Would you recommend this way of working to others as the best choice for employment?" A relatively high percentage of the respondents (between 40% and 50%) had no dilemma and answered in the affirmative. However, about 30% hesitated and said "maybe," and about a sixth said they would do so if it was the only choice offered. The percentage of those who said "no" was very small and ranged between 2.5% and 5.9%. Differences between countries are not statistically significant. Obviously, there is a division in which the first group is predominant, which has no doubt that it is the best form of employment and those who are ambivalent to varying degrees, but it should be noted that the percentage of those who are firmly for the negative option is more than 10 times for working from home as the best form of employment.

There are significant differences in the two factors. We applied *ANOVA*. On the first factor "Yes" is significantly more than "Maybe" ($I\text{–}J = 0.18932568$; $p = 0.009$) more than "No" ($I\text{–}J = 0.90865571$; $p = 0.000$)

"No" is significantly less than all: as we have seen less than "Yes," less than "Maybe" ($I\text{–}J = -0.71933003$; $p = 0.000$) and "I do not know, when it is the only choice" ($I\text{–}J = -0.74495546$; $p = 0.000$).

On the second factor, "Yes" is significantly higher than all the others; significantly more than "Maybe" ($I\text{–}J = 0.41272606$; $p = 0.000$) more than "No" ($I\text{–}J = 1.15334442$; $p = 0.000$) and higher than "I don't know, when it's the only choice" ($I\text{–}J = 0.64334929$; $p = 0.000$).

The respondents on the first factor, who cope well with psychosocial stresses (it should be constantly borne in mind that variables with negative signs are recoded—note B. Đ.) represent a predominantly affirmative attitude towards employment from home, although, as expected, it is more positive in the second factor because it includes variables that describe personal and professional fulfilment of work from home and satisfaction of a number of psychosocial needs.

The respondents in all four countries see the benefits of working from home, as mentioned by other authors (Allen, 2001; Baltes et al., 1999; Bloom et al., 2015; Gajenndran & Harisson, 2007; Greenhaus & Powell, 2006; Kurland & Baley, 1999; Thomas & Ganster, 1995) and only a very small number see no advantage. The main advantages are financial, because about a quarter believe that it is additional income that is realized through this work, and another fifth think that it is a permanent income. Immediately afterwards, on average, close to a third point out a longer stay together with their family, and close to a fifth believe that working from home establishes control over their own lives. The most significant difference is that the provision of permanent income is significantly more pronounced in Northern Macedonia than in BiH ($X2 = 60.394; p = 0.000$).

This result supports our earlier assumption that poor financial situation and unemployment are probably the main factors that those who do work from home are considered to be somewhat privileged and who therefore "overlook" some unfavorable aspects of this work, noted in other countries, or even see it through the pink glasses.

Statistically significant differences were found on both factors. In the first: significantly lower values are those who answered "Nothing" than those for whom working from home "Provides additional income" ($I–J = -0.02206212; p = 0.041$); "Nothing" significantly less than those who said, "More stays with family" ($I–J = -1.23760161; p = 0.013$).

Finally, in the first factor, those who said, "additional income is provided" have significantly lower values than those who said "permanent income is provided" ($I–J = 0.18660764; p = 0.047$). Further, those who said "additional income is provided" have significantly lower values than those who said that they stay with their family longer ($I–J = -0.20379749; p = 0.013$). The importance of a pleasant family environment is emphasized in the previously mentioned Indonesian study (Susilo, 2020).

In the other factor, those who said "nothing" have significantly less value than everyone else; significantly less than those who said, "additional income is provided ($I–J = -1,00711783; p = 0.043$); significantly less than those who said, "permanent income is provided" ($I–J = -1.03478527, p = 0.039$) and significantly less "of all the above" ($I–J = -1.98599372; p = 0.009$). Those who said "nothing" have significantly less value than those who said "establishing control over their own lives" ($I–J = -1.37547620; p = 0.000$); significantly less than those who said that they "spend more time with their family" ($I–J = -1.21091532; p = 0.015$) and significantly less than those who pointed out flexible working hours as the biggest advantage of working from home ($I–J = -1.40828646; p = 0.012$).

Those who said that working from home provided them with additional income had significantly less value than those who said that working from home gave them control over their own lives ($I–J$ = –0.36835836; p = 0.000) and significantly less than those who they said that since working from home they spend more time with family ($I–J$ = –0.20379749; p = 0.013). In addition to spending more time with family (Susilo et al., 2020), they emphasized the importance of achieving control over time and their own lives (Maruyama et al., 2009).

Finally, those who said that working from home provided them with a steady income had significantly less value than those who felt that working from home gave them control over their own lives ($I–J$ = –0.34069093; p = 0.000).

What can we conclude; the results from both factors first show that the respondents perceive through the benefits that working from home brings them, establish a kind of hierarchy among them in terms of importance that depends on the meaning that each factor has for them. What both factors have in common is a sharp polarization to those very few to whom work from home has brought nothing and everything else, and then polarizations to economic and other benefits. For those who managed to compensate for stressful psychosocial events on the first factor, probably thanks to the fact that work from home brought them greater financial security, they clearly showed that on this first factor as well, where the motives of greater financial achievement are more important than on the second factor.

Since the second factor highlighted respondents for whom working from home enabled not only full professional affirmation but also the satisfaction of a number of other needs, in their hierarchy of achievements more complex sociological and anthropological motives such as spending more time with family and, especially, better control over life, and then a more flexible distribution of time.

To the question "What should one be guided when starting a home-based business" on average close to a quarter of the respondents answered with a good business idea, and on average in similar percentages and reducing business costs due to renting office space, transportation costs, and so forth, the need to balance business and private life expectancy in BiH was on average in 39.3% of cases, in Montenegro and Northern Macedonia close to 22% and in Serbia close to 30%. In similar smaller percentages, the respondents were guided by higher earnings and employment of household members. Statistically significant differences were found among countries ($X2$ = 65,689; p = 0.000); in Montenegro, the most significant are different types of savings, and in BiH, balancing between business and private life. The rather uneven motive speaks of serious external obstacles to starting a home-based business, where a good business idea does not dominate.

Both factors are significant; the first ($F = 2.797$; $p = 0.011$) and the second ($F = 4.113$; $p = 0.000$).

In the first factor, "a good business idea" has higher values than "no investment in business premises, transportation, etc." (I-$J = 0.20496183$; $p = 0.022$) "desire to involve household members in the business" (I-$J = 0.45190286$; $p = 0.000$).

Desire to involve household members in the business is significantly less than "no investment in business premises, transportation, etc." (I-$J = -0.24694103$; $p = 0.041$) "balancing between business and private obligations" (I-$J = -.37665177$; $p = 0.002$) "higher income" (I-$J = -0.30808456$; $p = 0.020$).

In the second factor, a "good business idea" has significantly higher values than all answers, except for the answer "All of the above"; from the "Other" (I-$J = 0.66876856$; $p = 0.47$). "There are no investments in business premises, transportation, etc." (I-$J = 0.18686847$; $p = 0.037$). "The need for balancing between business and private obligations" (I-$J = 0.17662898$; $p = 0.041$) than "Higher earnings" (I-$J = 0.26958762$; $p = 0.010$) "Desire to involve household members in the work" (I-$J = 0.54776508$; $p = 0.000$).

Finally, the desire to involve household members in the business has less value than all, except for the "Other" answer; less than "Good business idea" (I-$J = -0.54776508$; $p = 0.000$) than "No investment in lease of business premises, transportation, etc." (I-$J = -0.36089661$; $p = 0.003$) than "the need for balancing between business and private obligations" (I-$J = -0.37113609$; $p = 0.000$) and from "Higher earnings" (I-$J = -0.27817746$; $p = 0.035$).

In the first factor, the respondents tend to balance more; although a good business idea is important, it is not as dominant as in the second factor, but it is "No investment ..." and "Balancing between private and business obligations," and so forth. In psychosocial stresses, with which the respondents successfully cope with the first factor, it should be taken into account that when deciding to start working from home, these respondents were faced with several challenges, which could certainly affect their greater caution what to give advantage to in the beginning and the effort to initially "go" on two or three tracks at the same time. Those who stood out on the second factor are more accomplished in the profession since they do work from home, which they are more willing to attribute to a "good business idea" due to raising self-esteem.

Only a tenth of the respondents in BiH and Serbia included other family members in their regular business activities, and in Montenegro and Northern Macedonia almost 22%. It is interesting to note that on average even more than a third of the family members of the respondents do not show any interest in getting involved, while slightly more than a fifth are satisfied with the advisory role. Finally, a little less than a fifth cannot do that because they do not have a contract with the employer. There are significant differences between the countries; the respondents from Northern Macedonia stated significantly less often that family members were "not interested for other reasons," and also from Montenegro significantly less stated that they were not interested, while family members from Serbia were significantly less interested in working at home ($X2 = 50.758$; $df = 15$; $p = 0.000$).

These differences may be due to less current jobs and lower payments in Montenegro and Northern Macedonia than in BiH, where the share of the IT sector and better paid jobs is relatively the highest, and the situation is similar in Serbia. Another reason is the weaker initial infrastructure for working from home and therefore the limited employment opportunities for more family members.

No statistically significant differences were found between countries by factors.

The following modalities stood out about the basic rules for successful business from home: training, workspace, previous experience, communication skills, and technical equipment.

When it comes to professional development, the differences between countries are highly significant; in BiH, professional training is favored by 55.2% of the respondents, and in Northern Macedonia by 25.8 ($X2 = 42.095$; $df = 3$; $p = 0.000$). This difference is not surprising because the structure by activity is the most favorable in BiH. Given the relatively large number of those working in the IT sector in BiH, continuous training is an imperative.

No statistically significant differences were found between countries by factors.

Workspace is important for over half of the respondents from Serbia and Macedonia for successful doing business from home, and for only a third of the respondents from BiH and Montenegro. The difference is statistically significant ($X2 = 23,671$; $df = 3$; $p = 0,000$). These differences are largely due to the type of activity; the respondents from BiH work on computers, and from Montenegro above average on education through platforms, which does not require a large working space, while the nature of activities from home in Serbia and Northern Macedonia is more polyvalent.

It is interesting to note that those who emphasize the importance of workspace have significantly higher scores on the first factor ($t = -3.512$; $p = 0.000$). It is possible that the respondents who compensated for unfavorable psychosocial factors were more frustrated by various external factors, including the narrowness of the workspace. Due to this unpleasant initial experience, they are more inclined to value the workspace more than others.

Previous experience as important for starting a home-based business was pointed out by over half of the respondents from Northern Macedonia and over two fifths from Serbia. In contrast, 19.9% of the respondents from BiH and 26.4% from Montenegro cited previous experience as significant. The difference is statistically highly significant ($X2 = 60.386$; $df = 3$; $p = 0.000$). The respondents from BiH work relatively briefly from home and find it more difficult to assess the importance of experience, and Montenegrins are probably less likely to attach more importance to experience given a range of routine work activities from home that do not require too much experience to gain.

Those who think that experience is important have higher scores on the second factor ($t = -3,201$; They are advocates of a good business idea as the key to doing business successfully from home, and for a good business idea experience is undoubtedly very important.

The respondents from Montenegro in almost three-fifths of cases believe that communication skills are not important for successful business and in two-fifths that they are important. We have a completely opposite relationship in the other three countries. The difference is statistically highly significant ($X2 = 21,373$; $df = 3$; $p = 0,000$).

The possible explanation is conditioned by cultural reasons; in Montenegro, informal family, friends, and similar relationships are probably more important for the success of a home-based business than good communication skills.

The respondents who agree that communication skills are significant have higher scores on the first factor ($t = -3,623$; $p = 0,000$). It is possible that the respondents who successfully compensated for various psychosocial stressful situations achieved this by developing communication skills. Kowalski and Swanson (2005) believe that training in communication skills is very important for successful remote.

When it comes to technical equipment as a precondition for a successful home-based business, again three-fifths of the respondents from Montenegro believe that it is not an important factor in running a successful home-based business, while two-fifths believe that it is. As in the previous case, the situation in the other three countries is completely reversed. The differences were statistically significant ($X2 = 28.704$; $df = 3$; $p = 0.000$). In this case, it is probably a matter of the classic rationalization "Technical equipment that I do not have or do not have quality equipment is not important enough then." These rationalizations are more prone to peoples who simply use the projective mechanism of negation on frustration in order to preserve the idealized image of themselves (see Table 4.7).

Table 4.7

The indicators of Successful Work From Home

The indicators of successfulness of working from home	Bosnia and-Herzegovina		Montene-gro		Northern Macedonia		Serbia		Total	
	N	%	N	%	N	%	N	%	N	%
Better balance of free and working time	89	44.3	57	28.4	34	15.4	100	24.5	280	27.2
Other	1	0.5	1	0.5	0	0.0	0	0.0	2	0.2
Longer stay with family	14	7.0	28	13.9	32	14.5	44	10.8	118	11.4
Business stress is reduced	47	23.4	44	21.9	27	12.7	65	15.9	183	17.7
All of the above	0	0.0	1	0.5	0	0.0	1	0.2	2	0.2
Higher earnings	28	13.9	34	16.9	77	34.8	143	35.0	282	27.4
Higher labor pro-ductivity	22	10.9	36	17.9	51	23.1	55	13.5	164	15.9
Total	201	100.0	201	100.0	221	100.0	408	100.0	1,031	100.0

Table 4.7. shows that for the respondents from all countries, a better balance of free and working time is the most important indicator of work success from home, as other authors point out (Jensen, 1994; Levis & Cooper, 2005; Mann et al., 2000). The exception is Northern Macedonia. Then comes higher earnings. However, when it comes to higher earnings, it is noticed that it is twice as important to the respondents from Serbia and Macedonia than to respondents from Montenegro, and when it comes to the respondents from BiH, two and a half times (Table 4.7). On the other hand, the reduction of business stress is a more important indicator of the success of work from home in BiH and Montenegro than in Serbia, and especially in Northern Macedonia. The importance of stress reduction is also pointed out by other authors (Montreuil & Lippel, 2003).

The difference can also be seen when it comes to the most frequent category—"better balance of free and working time," at least when it comes to BiH. All three differences reflect a kind of cultural models rather than stem from the built strategy in the organization of work from home. Namely, in Montenegro, and especially in BiH, the cultural-value elements of the Eastern cultural circle are more present than in Serbia and Macedonia, where success and efficiency are more measured by money, which is more reminiscent of the Protestant spirit. All four countries contain elements of both cultural circles, and this distinction should be understood very conditionally.

Differences between countries are statistically highly significant ($X2 = 102.623$; $df = 18$; $p = 0.000$). In BiH, significantly more as an indicator of success, they value a better balance of free and working time, better earnings significantly more in Serbia than in BiH, and significantly higher productivity in Northern Macedonia.

Significant differences were found on the first factor. Higher productivity is a significantly lower indicator of business success from home than a better balance of free and working time ($I–J = 0.36045091$; $p = 0.000$) length of stay with family ($I–J = -0.44378679$; $p = 0.000$) reduction of business stress ($I–J = -0.21219184$; $p = 0.047$) higher earnings ($I–J = -0.37543586$; $p = 0.000$) and it does not differ only from the category "other" and "everything else."

Finally, the category "reduced stress" on this factor is significantly less than the "length of stay with the family" ($I–J = -0.23159496$; $p = 0.048$), although the significance of the differences is almost on the border.

These findings are quite indicative because they implicitly indicate that overcoming stressful situations due to work from home is in various ways related to collectivist social patterns, which appear at least as precipitants, if not the causal factors of these stressful situations.

Contrary to some Western authors, who prefer productivity as a common denominator of successful remote work (Bailey & Kurland, 2002; Hackman & Oldman, 1976; Olson, 1989), remote workers in the Western Balkans predominantly prefer the importance of family support and advice from friends in reducing stress at work.

The question "How and under what conditions should an office be formed from home" is dominated by answers that indicate that this question is of secondary importance for the respondents; only on average more than 5% said that the office should be equipped as in any other company, and only 12.5% of the respondents from Northern Macedonia expressed such an attitude. In addition, on average, only 8.3% of the respondents point out ergonomic rules as important. On average, a little more than a fifth of the respondents think that whoever wants to work does not need a special space. However, more than a third (36.9%) believe that it is enough to provide space so that others do not disturb them, and only a quarter believe that space should be set aside within the house and an office should be created. The differences were statistically significant ($X2 = 48.649$; $df = 15$; $p = 0.000$).

The respondents from Northern Macedonia significantly more than others support the idea of arranging an office based on those outside the home, and the respondents from Montenegro significantly less than others support the idea that those who are motivated to work do not need special space.

Significant differences exist on the first factor ($F = 13.844$; $p = 0.000$).

The office should be equipped in the same way as in any other company, they corresponded significantly less to the category "other" $I-J = -1.31040130$; $p = 0.000$) or "whoever wants to work does not need special conditions ($I-J = -0.78028052$; $p = 0.000$) or "should provide a quiet space without the possibility of disturbance from the side ($I-J = -0.63292319$; $p = 0.000$) or "should single out a separate space within the house and make offices" ($I-J = -0.50443734$; $p = 0.000$). It does not differ significantly only in the ergonomic rules. Ergonomic rules as important for the formation of the office also stood out significantly less than the category "other" ($I-J = -1.30789391$; $p = 0.000$) less than "the one who wants to work does not need special conditions" ($I-J = -0.77777313$; $p = 0.000$) than the forming of a quiet space without the possibility of disturbance ($I-J = -0.63041580$; $p = 0.000$) and then the formation of a separate space within the house ($I-J = -0.50192995$; $p = 0.000$).

We can observe that the respondents are ambivalent on this factor. Although they declare the necessity of a particularly quiet and secluded space within the house, they consider it secondary in relation to motivation and commitment to work from home. Many do not even respect the necessity of respecting basic ergonomic rules. In our opinion, there are at least two reasons for this; burdened with the fulfilment of more important and urgent preconditions for good work than the office and ergonomic rules, the formation of the office comes in the third or fourth plan for implementation. The second is that many do not have the objective space and financial conditions to form a special office within the house, so they do not even think about it, but are satisfied with a secluded and peaceful corner if it is still possible to find it.

If we cannot agree that forming an office and respecting ergonomic rules is completely secondary to successful work from home, despite the existence of objective limitations, one can quite accept the explanation that self-motivation and self-confidence are key to starting and staying at remote work (Baruch, 2000; Morgan, 2004; Sullivan & Lewis, 2001).

When asked "How should you look and be dressed to do business from home?" most respondents considered this to be a peripheral and, ultimately, unimportant question. The answer "No need to dress up, which is the advantage of this job" was answered by an average of a quarter of the respondents, while on average more than two fifths (44.2%) said that it is not important how we look, but how well we work. Less than a fifth pointed out that the wardrobe should be adjusted to the type of work, and only an average of 6.1% said that they should look the same as going to the office.

There are significant differences between countries ($F = 8.493; p = 0.000$). In BiH, they say significantly more that "it doesn't matter what I look like, but how I work" and significantly more opt for the option that the wardrobe should not be adjusted to the type of work, while the respondents from Northern Macedonia point out that they should.

These results indicate that the mental image of the respondents in all countries is under a strong cultural stereotype that "a suit does not make a man." This stereotype has a strong cultural foundation in collectivist cultural patterns that a person receives confirmation and acceptance from the collectivity if he behaves in accordance with collective values and norms. Highlighting a person by appearance and dress is not acceptable. All this is contrary to the Western individualistic value concept, which includes numerous individual characteristics of those who enter the mental image of a successful entrepreneur who works from home. The first form of confirmation of this mental image is behavioral-appearance and dress.

The respondents gave ambivalent answers to the question "Should I be engaged in full-time or part-time work," which a third (32%) expressed by claiming that working from home is a job without working hours. That is why a quarter (28.2%) think that it is better to accept full-time work, and on average only 9.6% part-time. Ambivalence is also reflected in the answers of 28.7% of the respondents whether there is an alternative job on offer instead of work from home in additional or permanent time. The differences between countries are significant; the respondents from BiH point out significantly less that it is a job without working hours, and the respondents from Northern Macedonia and Serbia significantly more ($X2 = 90.860; df = 12; p = 0.000$). Further, the respondents from Northern Macedonia are significantly more willing to engage in additional working hours. Finally, the respondents from BiH pointed out significantly more that their decision on whether to engage in full-time or part-time work also depends on whether they have an alternative job on offer, while the respondents from Northern Macedonia were significantly less willing to accept the same option.

The differences are significant on both factors; on the first $F = 5.449$; $p = 0.000$, and on the second $F = 6.063; p = 0.000$.

"This is a job without working hours" is significantly more communicated than engaging in part-time work ($I–J = 0.45263635; p = 0.000$) full-time ($I–J = 0.18319345; p = 0.022$) than whether we have some other job ($I–J = 0.26827904; p = 0.001$).

Those who chose the "I would work full time" option would opt significantly more for that option than for the "I would work part time" option ($I–J = 0.26944290; p = 0.020$).

On the second factor, those who said, "I don't know" significantly less opted for the option "work without working hours" $I–J = -0.82275562$;

$p = 0.002$) in additional working hours ($I\text{--}J = -0.58076528$; $p = 0.035$) full time ($I\text{--}J = -0.95711181$; $p = 000$) and for the option "depends if there is another job" ($I\text{--}J = 0.71578861$; $p = 0.006$).

The respondents who opted for the "I would work full time" option on the second factor would opt significantly more for that option than those who said "I don't know" ($I\text{--}J = 0.95711181$; $p = 0.000$) who would work in additional working hours ($I\text{--}J = 0.37634653$; $p = 0.000$) and from those who said "It depends if there is another job" ($I\text{--}J = 0.24132320$; $p = 0.003$).

Finally, the respondents who chose the "The job without working hours" option chose this option significantly more than the "I don't know" option ($I\text{--}J = 0.82275562$; $p = 0.002$) or the "I would work overtime" option ($I\text{--}J = 0.24199034$; $p = 0.033$).

The choice of the option "This is a job without working hours," which appeared as the most common choice in a third of cases, significantly relativizes all other options and affects increased ambivalence, which is seen by the fact that it is better to work full time than part time. The degree of ambivalence can also be seen in the respondents' choices on the second factor where the "I don't know" option is dominant. Finally, ambivalence is reflected in the fact that on average more than a quarter answered, "It depends if there is another job."

Expressed ambivalence is conditioned by at least two mutually opposing factors; psychophysical burdens due to a job for which neither the time nor the result is known in advance, and the fear of losing such a job if one does not agree to such conditions.

In this case, there is a discrepancy between our employees from home and the experiences of Western countries, where employees prefer additional work that allows them flexible working hours. This is understandable if it is known that new modalities of remote work have a longer tradition in Western countries and are better organized and institutionalized, especially when it comes to legal aspects.

The respondents use different strategies to increase earnings, but to a very different extent. The type and scope of the measures they use seem to be conditioned by the time available (when they usually do not have enough) and also limited financial resources, and not infrequently by real needs. They often do not use more complex strategies due to limited time and financial resources, and often out of the belief that simpler and more accessible strategies are sufficient for them to do their job successfully. Certainly, the complexity and scope of strategies are significantly influenced by the type of activity, which will already be shown in the following percentage structures. As expected, exchanging experiences with other colleagues from the same industry is the most accessible, simplest and at the same time cheapest strategy. It is practiced by an average of 29.5% of the respondents. The second most represented is the monitoring of professional literature, on average 18.6%. The respondents from BiH deviate significantly from this average, and in 25.9% of cases they constantly follow the professional literature. If it is known that in this sample there is an above-average number of those who work in the IT sector and programmers, it is certainly that following the professional and scientific literature is the fastest and cheapest way to get new information to improve your work from home. With the respondents from Serbia, they are the most numerous among those who improve their work from home by exchanging experiences with colleagues from the same industry. Unlike others, they can only be referred to them.

Expert advice is used by an average of 13.9% of the respondents, except for the respondents from Northern Macedonia who deviate more than twice from that average—29.4%. Significantly greater focus on experts in Northern Macedonia is due to the relatively higher representation of some activities, especially in industry and education, which to a greater extent include expert advice in order to improve work from home.

Going to professional seminars in order to obtain professional certificates occupy a peripheral place with only 8.3%. This seems to be due to the considerable routine nature of work done from home and insufficient involvement in global processes, as a result of which the acquisition of these professional certificates is for most more a matter of personal prestige than a necessary condition for improving business from home.

On average, more than a quarter (28.6%) do not have a special strategy for improving earnings, which, in our opinion, is due to the aforementioned reasons—the unfavorable structure of activities performed from home, their routine and insufficient involvement in modern global social, economic and technological processes.

The differences between the countries are highly statistically significant, the possible causes of which we have tried to point out somewhat earlier. The respondents from Northern Macedonia rely significantly more than others on expert advice, and significantly less on exchanging experiences with long-term colleagues from the same industry, while the respondents from BiH rely mostly on professional literature in order to improve their work from home and earnings.

There are significant differences in both factors. On the first $F = 5.449$; $p = 0.000$ and on the other $F = 6.063$; $p = 0.000$.

On the first factor for "I rely on the advice of experts" they opt significantly more than for 'I' go to professional seminars and get professional certificates" $(I–J = 0.42417547; p = 0.002)$ "I do not have a special strategy $(I–J = 0.53999077; p = 0.000)$ "I exchange experiences with other colleagues from the same industry" $(I–J = 0.31310974; p = 0.002)$ "I constantly follow the professional literature and receive additional education" $(I–J = 0.48032980; p = 0.000)$.

The respondents on this factor who said they did not have a specific strategy relied significantly less on expert advice ($I\!-\!J = -0.5399977$; $p =0.000$) significantly less exchanged experiences with colleagues from the same industry ($I\!-\!J =-0.22688103$; $p = 0.005$).

On the other factor, those who do not have a specific strategy significantly less rely on expert advice ($I\!-\!J = -0.38636549$; $p =0.000$) significantly less exchange experiences with colleagues from the same industry ($I\!-\!J = -0.28991582$; $p = 0.000$) and significantly they follow the professional literature less and are additionally educated ($I\!-\!J = -0.22559428$; $p = 0.014$).

The respondents on the first factor seem to have somewhat less self-confidence to increase earnings from home and therefore seek more support from professional authorities. Further, their strategies are less clearly profiled and consistent because, as opposed to those who seek expert advice, there are others who have the opposite strategy.

The finding on the second factor is completely unexpected, because it is on it that we should expect developed and designed strategies for increasing the earnings of businesses from home. The only possible explanation is that they have achieved privileged positions in the business on various legal and semilegal grounds, of which there can be many, and then their strategies are almost irrelevant.

Table 4.8

The Most Common Problems in Running a Home-Based Business

The most common problems in running a home-based business	Bosnia and Herzegovina		Montenegro		Northern Macedonia		Serbia		Total:	
	N	%	N	%	N	%	N	%	N	%
Other	2	1.0	1	0.5	0	0.0	5	1.2	8	0.8
Monotony in doing work that leads to depression	17	8.5	24	11.9	20	9.0	47	11.5	108	10.5
Lack of social communication	34	16.9	41	20.4	58	26.2	67	16.4	200	19.4
No special problems	53	26.4	52	25.9	89	40.3	181	44.4	375	36.4
It is over-worked. i.e. until the job is done.	42	20.9	38	18.9	28	12.7	64	15.7	172	16.7

(Table continued on next page)

Table 4.8 (Continued)

The Most Common Problems in Running a Home-Based Business

The most com-mon problems in running a home-based business	Bosnia and Herze-govina		Montenegro		Northern Macedonia		Serbia		Total	
	N	%	N	%	N	%	N	%	N	%
It is difficult to separate business from private obliga-tions.	53	26.4	45	22.4	26	11.8	44	10.8	168	16.3
Total	201	100.0	201	100.0	221	100.0	408	100.0	1,031	100.0

Table 4.8 shows that the respondents state various problems in running a home-based business. However, the problems that dominate foreign research, such as monotony, do not come to the fore in our respondents. The lack of social communication is relatively most pronounced (especially in Northern Macedonia), and the excessive workload and the inability to separate business from private obligations occur in almost identical percentages. Our sample is separated from others by an above-average percentage of those who said that they have no special problems due to working from home. The inability to be excluded from work due to overload is also significant in foreign research (Felstead & Henseke, 2017). However, the most frequently mentioned and most serious problem is the separation of business and family obligations and finding a balance between them (Lewis & Cooper, 2005; Kreiner et al., 2009). In one large survey, 60% of employees report that breaking boundaries is the most difficult problem at home (Ellison, 1999). Conflicts, which due to the collapse of the boundaries between work and family, lead to the most difficult consequences such as burnout (Allvin et al., 2011; Lingard & Francis, 2006; Noonan & Glas, 2012).

Countries differ significantly by type of problem due to work at home ($X2 = 65.398$; $df = 15$; $p = 0.000$). The respondents from Northern Macedonia are significantly more likely to feel the lack of social communication due to work at home, while the respondents from BiH and Montenegro are less likely to have special problems, and the respondents from Serbia are significantly more aware of this problem. Finally, the respondents from BiH say more than others that it is difficult for them to separate business from private obligations.

There are significant differences in both factors; on the first $F = 50.775$; $p = 0.000$ and on the second $F = 8.443$; $p = 0.000$.

On the first factor, the respondents who answered "other" experience significantly less monotony at work (I–J = 1,11338250; p = 0.001) significantly less feel a lack of social communication (I–J = 0.86962958; p = 0.007) overwork significantly less (I–J = 1.17466787; p = 0.000) have significantly fewer problems separating business from private obligations (I–J = 1.22195281; p = 0.000).

Those who suffered from monotony while working from home responded significantly less with "other" (I–J = –1,11338250; p = 0.001) and they significantly less socially communicated while working from home (I–J = –0.24375292; p = 0.023) and significantly less pointed out that they had no special problems (I–J = –0.91573860; p = 0.000).

The respondents who pointed out the lack of social communication while working from home said significantly more that they had no special problems (I–J = 0.67198568; p = 0.000) and significantly more that it was difficult for them to separate business from private obligations (I–J = 0.35232323; p = 0.000). Those who did not have special problems pointed out significantly more overwork (I–J = 0.97702397; p = 0.000) and pointed out significantly more that it is difficult to separate business from private obligations (I–J = 1.02430891; p = 0.000).

On the second factor, the respondents who pointed out monotony while working from home experienced significantly less lack of social communication (I–J = –0.30916621; p = 0.008). At the same time, they significantly less often pointed out that they have no special problems (I–J = –0.64282764; p = 0.000) and significantly less opted for the option "overtime work" (I–J = –0.38979212; p = 0.001) and for the option "difficult is to separate business from private obligations. "

Finally, the respondents who said "No special problems" significantly more than others opted for the "other" option (I–J = 0.69493864; p = 0.048) emphasized monotony at home (I–J = 0.64282764; p = 0.000) lack of social communication (I–J = 0.33366143; p = 0.000) and overtime work (I–J = 0.25303552; p = 0.005).

The results on both factors are quite contradictory. Only at first glance this contradiction should be attributed to the insincerity of the respondents. They become "understandable" and "logical" if placed in a broader social context of high unemployment and therefore chronic frustration in meeting often basic biological, and especially more complex social and cultural needs. Only in this context do the paradoxical conclusions that there are no special problems become understandable, and then a number of different problems stand out. However, the fact that they are employed (even temporarily) makes the respondents feel privileged, especially if they earn above-average salaries as freelancers. The very fact that their psychophysical efforts to earn those salaries on average far exceed those salaries, especially if they are compared to similar jobs in Western countries, is not particularly important to them because they cannot influence its change. For these reasons, our respondents minimize problems and the entire *mise-en-scène* of work from home tends to paint pinker than it actually is.

Although based on these results it is difficult to assess which of the problems are the most difficult to solve for the respondents, it seems that these are still difficulties in separating business and private obligations. The question is, Why? As we have seen on the basis of the results of foreign research, they subsume through other problems, and represent their kind of common denominator, which for example, includes lack of time for recreational activities and hobbies, reduced social communication, difficulties in organizing and fulfilling planned professional and other activities, more stereotypes and routines in their execution than we would like, loss of self-confidence, feelings of isolation and abandonment, depersonalization and, finally, burnout.

In the use of strategies for overcoming problems, there is a lack of adequate strategies and attempts to compensate for this with emotional relaxation in the circle of family and friends. In fact, only two strategies allow for direct problem-facing and problem-solving, while others are either inadequate or can only indirectly contribute to problem-facing and problem-solving. Those two strategies are: going to meetings and seminars and meeting with associates once a week. On average it is a quarter of them—25.3%.

In an average of 17.1% of cases, the respondents point out that they simply do not know what they could do because the alienation of those who work from home is great, which is why they are ready to seek the help of a psychologist.

All the other seek support and help from family members and friends—56.1%. This support and assistance is the most sought in Serbia (64.7%) and BiH (61.2%) and least in Montenegro (41.8%).

The differences are statistically highly significant ($X2 = 79.711$; $df = 18$, $p = 0.000$). The respondents ask for significantly less support and help for their problems at work from home in Montenegro, and significantly more in Serbia and BiH. At the same time, the respondents from Montenegro are looking for a significantly better solution to problems at work at home by going to professional meetings and seminars. In this case, similar cultural patterns operate in different ways due to specific ethnopsychological reasons in Montenegro in relation to Serbia and BiH. In Montenegro, patriarchal family patterns are more controlling and punishing, which is why even in performing daily routines, an individual engages with less self-confidence and fearfully seeks help from the collective out of fear and anxiety that the collectivity can be marginalized as more or less unworthy of ethical and value collectivist patterns. In Serbia and BiH, such restrictive patterns are significantly less prevalent, which is why people in trouble are more likely to seek support and help from primary groups, without much fear and anxiety that they will be marginalized or rejected. However, this example also points us to the positive side of the coin—consciously, and more often unconsciously fleeing from an anachronistic cultural pattern, the respondents from Montenegro turn to mature social solutions above average; 20.4% of the respondents participate in professional meetings and seminars, 8% in BiH and 7.1% in Serbia. However, this increased percentage of participants from Montenegro can be partly attributed to the above-average representation of educational profiles of those who work from home in Montenegro, which include permanent education through professional gatherings and seminars.

Finally, what practical advice would home business owners give to future entrepreneurs when they had the chance. Our respondents largely agree on the content of practical advice, and even their order. As expected, a good business plan is in the first place—33.7%. However, it should be noted that the percentage is highest in BiH (38.3%) followed by Serbia (37%) while it is the lowest in Montenegro (27.4%) and Northern Macedonia (29%). Similar percentage structures exist in the other two strategies, which assume that we treat work at home as responsibly as we do work outside home, as well as the imperative of continuous professional development (see Table 4.8). The need to constantly consult with experts for every aspect of the job whenever necessary is still significantly less represented in percentage—on average only 9.8%.

The differences between countries are statistically significant ($X2 = 41.120$; $df = 12$, $p = 0.000$). Proponents of a good business plan are significantly more represented in BiH than in Montenegro, and the need to consult with experts whenever we have a problem is significantly more present in Northern Macedonia than in BiH.

Significant differences were found only in the first factor ($F = 4.674$; $p = 0.001$). Those who point out a good business plan are significantly more represented than those who recommend continuous professional development ($I\text{–}J = 0.29235409$; $p = 0.000$) and those who recommend future entrepreneurs to consult for every aspect of the job, whenever necessary ($I\text{–}J = 0.31894538$; $p = 0.005$).

The proponents of the strategy of not distinguishing between work at home and away from home are significantly more represented than those who insist on continuous professional development ($I\text{–}J = 0.24003574$; $p = 0.004$) or on constant consultations with professionals for every aspect of their work, whenever necessary ($I\text{–}J = 0.26662703$; $p = 0.019$).

The prevailing strategies are a good business plan and commitment to that plan, which are obviously both the most important and probably the

best strategies that home business owners can recommend to future entrepreneurs (see Table 4.9).

Table 4.9

Practical Advice From Home Business Owners to Future
Entrepreneurs

Practical advice from business owners from home to future entrepreneurs	BiH		Montene-gro		Northern Macedonia		Serbia		Total	
Other	4	2.0	1	0.5	0	0.0	4	1.0	9	0.9
Make a good business plan and learn to manage your time.	77	38.3	55	27.4	64	29.0	151	37.0	347	33.7
Do not make a distinction between the work you do from home and those abroad.	65	32.3	69	34.3	54	24.4	118	28.9	306	29.7
Constantly improve yourself professionally	50	24.9	58	28.9	66	29.9	94	23.0	268	26.0
Always consult with experts for every aspect of your job whenever necessary.	5	2.5	18	9.0	37	16.7	41	10.0	101	9.8
Total	201	100.0	201	100.0	221	100.0	408	100.0	1031	100.0

The Influence of Freelancing on the Psychosocial Adjustment to Work From Home

Freelancers are the most numerous and significant group of those who
work from home. As we have seen, changes in the way of working, which
due to the work across the platforms presuppose constant adaptation to
new technological innovations, are neither the most important nor the
most numerous preconditions for the successful freelancing. The psychological adjustment to freelancing is more challenging and more numerous
in changing. That is why in this chapter we tried to examine how our
respondents in the mentioned four countries of the Western Balkans adapt
psychosocially to different aspects of freelance. Before that, we will show
the representation of freelancing in those four countries.

By testing factor scores with the *t*-test, we found that there are statistically significant differences in the first factor ($t = -3.726$; $p = 0.000$). Namely, nonfreelancers have a significantly lower score on the first factor. If we recall that the responses were recoded then we come to the conclusion that nonfreelancers are exposed to greater psychosocial stresses than freelancers.

When asked "What is most important to you when choosing a job," no statistically significant differences were found between countries. However, it should be mentioned that the most important thing for the respondents from BiH is flexible working hours (40.3%). That is because flexible working hours are a prerequisite and a common denominator for achieving a number of positive benefits of working from home (autonomy and freedom, motivation, good planning of daily activities, establishing boundaries between work and private life, etc.) and it is emphasized by almost all authors (Ford & Butts, 1991; Wienclav, 2019). Good earnings are important to all the other countries (Montenegro—44.4%, Northern Macedonia—42%, and Serbia—44%). Job training comes at the end and is mentioned by a quarter of the respondents, relatively the most in Serbia and BiH.

No statistically significant differences were found by factor scores.

If working in the "Gig Economy" was the only job, 76.5% of the respondents from Serbia answered that they would accept such a job, and 49.6% of the respondents from BiH. The difference is statistically significant; the respondents from BiH would significantly less often accept freelance as the only source of income, and significantly less often than others if it were the only option ($X2 = 30.192$; $df = 6$; $p = 0.000$).

Statistically significant differences were found in the second factor ($F = 10.301$; $p = 0.000$). In other words, those who meet their professional aspirations, financial and other social needs through freelancing are much more willing to work in the "Gig Economy" as the only source of income.

There are significant differences on the second factor; the respondents who met their professional, financial, and social needs were significantly less likely to work in the "Gig Economy" as a hobby or as a volunteer ($F = 3.777$; $p = 0.024$).

When asked "Would they change their full-time employment for a flexible contract job," 51.2% of the respondents from BiH said "yes" and only 34% from Serbia, while as many as 65.6% of the respondents from Serbia said either "No" or that they just wanted a secure job. However, no statistically significant differences were found between countries in this regard.

Differences exist on the first factor; the respondents who are not exposed to psychosocial stresses due to working from home significantly more often prefer only a secure job ($F = 7.198$; $p = 0.001$). Obviously, the possible temptations associated with precarious employment status are the main reason for choosing only a secure and permanent job.

The respondents from BiH in the last two years have worked significantly more for two to five employers, and from Serbia over 5 ($X2 = 19.519$; $df = 9$; $p = 0.021$). In addition, there are statistically significant differences in both factors; in the first ($F = 11.607$; $p = 0.000$) and in the second ($F = 3.208$; $p = 0.019$). In the first factor, those who worked for two to five employers have a lower score than the other two options. Those who had fewer psychosocial problems due to working at home were less willing to change employers, and those who were more satisfied with their jobs and the fulfilment of their other life needs were more willing to change employers or were left with only one. If they stayed at one, they were obviously satisfied with it, and if they changed more than five, they had higher expectations from employers. In any case, they were more willing to change than the respondents without psychosocial problems due to working from home.

The next question refers to the type of jobs that the respondents did in the "Gig Economy" in the last two years. These were: programming, translation, teaching, research.

In BiH, 38% are engaged in programming, and in Montenegro 15.6%. The difference is statistically significant ($X2 = 10.971$; $df = 3$; $p = 0.012$). No statistically significant differences were found by factors.

No significant differences were found between countries in terms of translation representation. However, it was observed that those who did not work on translation had a higher score on the second factor ($t = 2.336$; $p = 0.02$). This result might suggest the assumption that translation is a more stressful activity than some others, but it can be more reliably concluded based on other research.

Seventy-eight percent of the respondents practice lectures at home in BiH, 30.5% in Macedonia and 28.9% in Serbia. The difference is statistically highly significant ($X2 = 25.430$; $df = 3$; $p = 0.000$). Lectures from home are practiced significantly more in Macedonia and Serbia, and significantly less in BiH. No significant differences were found in both factors.

Twenty-six percent of respondents in BiH and 43.5% in Northern Macedonia participate in the research. The difference is statistically significant ($X2 = 9.403$; $df = 3$; $p = 0.024$).

In the first factor, those who participate in research have a higher score ($t = -1.993$; $p = 0.047$). This finding is on the verge of statistical significance. In the second factor, those who do not participate have a higher score ($t = -2.331$, $p = 0.020$). For those who do not have psychosocial problems due to work from home, research provides additional motivation for professional affirmation, and especially for those who have already achieved professional affirmation and satisfaction of a number of other life needs thanks to work from home.

No statistically significant differences were found among freelancers who performed "other tasks" from home. However, it should be mentioned that about one sixth of the respondents from BiH practice other jobs, and about a quarter from three other countries. The reason is certainly in the fact that the respondents from BiH work significantly more often in programming and in the IT sector. Given a number of advantages, they have less needs and motivation to look for other and additional jobs.

On both factors, those who do not do other jobs have higher scores; on the first ($t = 4.404; p = 0.000$) and on the second ($t = 2.092; p = 0.038$). This finding is in itself expected since constant surfing on platforms and looking for new jobs is a determinant of freelance. The second reason should be sought in the fact that freelancers do not have pronounced psychosocial problems due to work from home and in "other jobs" they find additional motivation to satisfy various professional aspirations. Those who have satisfied their professional aspirations, material, and social needs with existing work from home by taking on "other jobs" are trying to expand and strengthen these professional benefits.

The next question is about the benefits of working from home via platforms. These include life, health, pension insurance and none of that.

When it comes to life insurance, it is noticed that this insurance has a very small percentage of the respondents in all countries; 7.8% in BiH, 11.1% in Montenegro, 9.2% in Northern Macedonia and 6.6% in Serbia. The differences between countries are not statistically significant.

As expected, those who do not have health insurance have a higher score in the first factor. The lack of that insurance intensifies the anxiety from the possible occurrence of psychosocial problems after a long period of work.

It is worrying that in all four countries, on average, only a quarter (24.8%) have health insurance; in BiH, 21.7% of freelancers have health insurance, in Montenegro 35.6%, in Northern Macedonia 36.6% and in Serbia only 15.1%. Montenegro and Northern Macedonia have significantly more health insured persons among freelancers, and Serbia significantly less ($X2 = 21.722; p = 0.000$).

A higher score was recorded for both factors; in the first ($t = 3.825; p = 0.000$) and in the second ($t = 2.832; p = 0.005$). We could repeat the earlier explanation; for those who are under increased mental and health tensions (the first factor), the lack of health insurance creates additional tension and tension, and those who are professionally, financially and socially satisfied with working from home feel the need to achieve even greater financial benefits to create additional funding for self-financing of own treatment, if necessary.

The data when it comes to pension insurance are also very worrying; in BiH, pension insurance was provided by only 7.8% of the respondents, in Montenegro by 31.1%, in Northern Macedonia by 29% and in Serbia by 16.3%. In Montenegro and Northern Macedonia, they exercised significantly more of the right to pension insurance, and less in BiH, and even in Serbia ($X2 = 24.324$; $df = 3$; $p = 0.000$).

Those who do not have pension insurance have a higher score on both factors; in the first ($t = 3,337$; $p = 0.001$) and on the second ($t = 2.692$; $p = 0.007$). The possible explanation is the same as in the case of health insurance.

Finally, it is very surprising that significant percentages of freelancers in all four countries did not receive any type of insurance, although the differences between countries are still significant. Thus, 71.3% of freelancers in BiH did not have any insurance, 44.4% in Montenegro 59, 5% in Northern Macedonia and even 78.9% in Serbia. There are significantly fewer freelancers in Montenegro who did not obtain any insurance than in Serbia ($X2 = 25.584$; $df = 3$; $p = 0.000$).

The next question is: "What aspects of life has your participation in the Gig Economy' negatively affected?" Four modalities stood out: professionally, privately, it did not have a negative impact, it affected financially. The vast majority of freelancers said there were no negative consequences for their professional engagements—more than 95% in all four states. It is expected that then the differences cannot be statistically significant. Satisfaction with freelancers is also expressed by freelancers in other studies (Burke, 2015).

Significant differences were found only in the first factor; freelancers who did not have negative consequences had higher scores in the first factor ($F = 3.356$; $p = 0.001$). The conclusion is common sense; if they did not have professional problems due to work from home there was no basis for stressful situations either.

On average, four-fifths of freelancers pointed out that participation in the "Gig Economy" had no negative consequences in their private lives, with the exception of Serbia, where that percentage is around three quarters. No statistically significant differences were found between countries.

The freelancers who do not have private problems have higher scores in both factors.

About three quarters of freelancers pointed out that working in the "Gig Economy" did not have negative consequences in their lives (68.9 in Montenegro and 69.3 in Serbia). The differences between countries are not statistically significant. This job satisfaction in the "Gig Economy" is also reported by other researchers (Baruch, 2000; Morgan, 2004). Higher scores occurred in both factors; $t = .519$ ($p = 0.000$ in the first and $t = 5.047$; $p = 0.000$ in the second. As expected, the respondents who do not have psychosocial problems and are satisfied with work, financially and socially have significantly fewer problems due to working from home.

In a very high percentage, which ranged between 95% and 100%, the freelancers in all four countries pointed out that they did not have financial problems due to their work in the "Gig Economy." No statistically significant differences were found using the X2 test. Freelancers who did not have financial problems had higher scores in the second factor (t = 3.066; p = 0.006). This is quite expected because satisfaction with the financial situation is part of another factor's composite. Although in other research, the freelancers pointed out their satisfaction with freelance, they still more often pointed out the problems they encountered while dealing with freelance (Burke, 2015). We have already said that employees from home and freelancers are prone to paint the shortcomings of remote work in pink.

The answers to the following two questions show that freelancers are more critical.

In the next question, the freelancers were asked about the positive impacts of their work in the "Gig Economy" in the same areas. In assessing the positive contribution in the profession, however, the freelancers were significantly more moderate than they reported on the negative professional impact. Fifty-one percent of the freelancers in BiH, 43.5% in Macedonia, 57.8% in Serbia and only 28.9% in Montenegro see positive contributions to work in the "Gig Economy." The differences were statistically significant ($X2$ = 14.443; df = 3; p = 0.002). The freelancers see the least positive contributions in Montenegro, and the most in Serbia.

The freelancers have significantly higher scores in the second factor (t = 4.556; p = 0.000). It is quite expected and logical for freelancers to assess the positive professional contributions of working in the "Gig Economy" if it has enabled them to achieve important professional goals and the realization of a number of important social needs.

Let us recall that about four-fifths of the freelancers pointed out that their engagement in the "Gig Economy" did not have negative consequences for their private lives. However, in similar percentages (with the exception of Montenegro) they stated that there were no positive ones; thus, 73.6% of the freelancers in BiH said that they did not have a positive impact on their private life, 86.3% in Macedonia, 74.7% in Serbia, and the most positive were the freelancers in Montenegro—57.8%. In Montenegro significantly more and in Northern Macedonia significantly less ($X2$ = 16.302; p = 0.001).

The freelancers who have positive changes in their private lives due to working in the "Gig Economy" have higher scores in the second factor. The explanation is similar to the previous case.

In BiH, there were only 0.8% of the freelancers who said that their work in the "Gig Economy" did not have a positive impact, and in Montenegro 11.1%, the differences are statistically significant; significantly more of them assessed the work in the "Gig Economy" in a negative context than in BiH ($X2$ = 10.737; df = 3; p = 0.013).

The freelancers who believe that working in the "Gig Economy" had a positive effect on them have a higher score in the first factor ($t = 2.280$; $p = 0.026$). It is logical to assume that freelancers who evaluated their work in the "Gig Economy" more positively had less psychosocial stress because of that than the freelancers who had negative experiences in that regard.

As in the previous case, the freelancers generally pointed out more often that working in the "Gig Economy" did not have negative financial consequences than they pointed out positive financial gains, although it should be noted that these financial benefits still stood out in high percentages. Thus, these positive benefits were emphasized by 76% in BiH, 80.9% in Northern Macedonia, 86.7% in Serbia, and only 46.7% in Montenegro. The freelancers from Montenegro assessed the financial contributions of work in the "Gig Economy" significantly more negatively, and significantly more positively from Serbia ($X2 = 34.463$; $p = 0.000$). It seems that the financial benefits were the most important, which is why the freelancers generally evaluated their engagement in freelance very positively.

The freelancers had higher scores in both factors, saying that working in the "Gig Economy" had a positive effect on their finances; in the first factor $t = -2,770$; $p = 0.006$ and in the second $t = -2.748$; $p = 0.013$. Certainly, financial benefits are important factors in easier coping with stressful situations in any job, even working in the "Gig Economy," which can explain this first result, while the positive financial effects are part of the composite of the second factor.

Asked whether working in the "Gig Economy" could significantly reduce unemployment in more than two-thirds of cases, they said yes; and only about 6% had negative attitudes about reducing unemployment while the rest were undecided (in about a quarter of cases). However, the freelancers from Montenegro have more negative attitudes than everyone else; as many as 26.7% believe that working in the "Gig Economy" cannot reduce unemployment, and 24.4% said they did not know. The freelancers from Montenegro said "no" significantly more often than everyone else ($X2 = 23.772$; $df = 6$; $p = 0.001$). Significantly higher scores were found in both factors. In the first, "no" is less than "yes" and "I don't know" ($I-J = -0.38245704$; $p = 0.019$). Further, in the first "no" is less than "I don't know" ($I-J = -0.41821543$; $p = 0.019$). In the second, "yes" is more than "no" ($I-J = 0.47955380$; $p = 0.004$) and "yes" more than "I don't know" ($I-J = 0.37055410$; $p = 0.000$). The freelancers who had less psychosocial stress were more inclined to look more optimistically at the possibility of reducing unemployment by introducing the "Gig Economy," and the freelancers who achieved a number of professional aspirations, material and social needs are even more optimistic in this regard.

When asked "Does working in the" Gig Economy" contributes to the quality of life?" only about 5% of the freelancers said that working in the

"Gig Economy" did not contribute to the quality of life. The freelancers from Montenegro in 13.3% of cases gave a negative assessment that working in the "Gig Economy" can improve the quality of life. In addition, in more than a quarter of cases, the freelancers from Montenegro were indecisive, and in the other three countries about a fifth. However, the differences between Montenegro and the other three countries do not reach the level of statistical significance.

Significantly higher scores were found in both factors. The first has "yes" significantly more than "no" ($I\text{--}J = 0.67932381$; $p = 0.001$) and "yes" more than "I don't know" ($I\text{--}J = 0.28681511$; $p = 0.009$). The second has "yes" more than "no" ($I\text{--}J = 2052653$; $p = 0.000$) and "yes" more than "I don't know" ($I\text{--}J = 0.49274567$; $p = 0.000$). Based on positive experiences with working from home, freelancers are ready to extend the improvement of the quality of life to other areas of life in the first factor (and especially in the second).

There were no statistically significant differences in the attitudes of the freelancers in the four countries on improving the position of workers in the "Gig Economy." Nevertheless, it should be noted that the freelancers from Montenegro more often emphasized the strengthening of legal legislation (57.8%) and the freelancers from BiH more often insist on strengthening the trust of employers towards freelancers, in order to more easily extend the employment contract (40.3%).

There are no significant differences by factors (see Table 4.10).

Table 4.10

Can Working Across Pplatforms and in the "Gig Economy" Reduce Brain Drain Abroad?

	Bosnia and Herzegovina		Montenegro		Northern Macedonia		Serbia		Total	
	N	%	N	%	N	%	N	%	N	%
Can working across platforms and in the "Gig Economy" reduce the brain drain abroad? Yes	94	72.9	19	42.2	86	65.6	90	54.2	289	61.4
No	15	11.6	17	37.8	5	3.8	16	9.6	53	11.3
I do not know	20	15.5	9	20.0	40	30.5	60	36.1	129	27.4
Total	129	100.0	45	100.0	131	100.0	166	100.0	471	100.0

The differences among the freelancers in the four states are statistically highly significant ($X2 = 54.887$; $df = 6$; $p = 0.000$). The freelancers from BiH say significantly more "yes" and the freelancers from Northern Macedonia significantly less "no," from Serbia significantly more "I don't know," from Montenegro significantly more "no." Basically, the freelancers from BiH and Northern Macedonia have two thirds (Northern Macedonia) and over 70% (BiH) of positive beliefs that working through platforms in the "Gig Economy" will reduce the brain drain abroad, the freelancers from Serbia are significantly more likely than others indecisive, and from Montenegro significantly more often do not believe in reducing brain drain (Table 4.10).

The dominant optimistic picture can also be seen in the factor scores, which are significant in both factors. Namely, those who said "No" ($I–J = -0.39169951$; $p = 0.006$) and "I don't know" than "Yes" ($I–J = 0.49974058$; $p = 0.001$) have significantly lower scores in the first factor. In the second factor, they said "Yes" significantly more often than "No" ($I–J = 0.55806601$; $p = 0.000$) and "I don't know" ($I–J = -0.57015098$; $p = 0.000$). We can conclude that in both factors, the freelancers actually had a primarily optimistic picture, more pronounced in the other factor. This is to be expected, since the freelancers who stood out in the second factor have stronger experiences of professional fulfilment and success, associated with working in the "Gig Economy."

Four Sociopsychological Profiles of Psychosocial Adjustment to Work From Home and Differences Among Them

Based on quantitative indicators, we will describe the most important qualitative features of psychosocial adjustment in the four countries and point out possible differences.

Then, based on quantitative indicators, we will perform a qualitative analysis of similarities and differences in terms of adjustment to the economic aspects of working from home in four countries.

Finally, based on quantitative indicators, we will point out the qualitative differences and similarities of freelance in the four countries of the Western Balkans.

All of these analyses will be integrated within a separate home-working profile for each of the four Western Balkan countries.

Bosnia and Herzegovina

As in other countries, the respondents from Bosnia and Herzegovina who work from home do not differ significantly, while they are the youngest population by age. They have significantly lower education than all the others, especially than the respondents from Serbia and Montenegro. By type of activity, they work significantly more than all others in the IT sector as developers.

According to a number of characteristics, the respondents from BiH are relatively well adapted to work from home; they leave enough time for their free activities and hobbies, although sometimes they lack time for physical activities. They have no problems with the quantity and quality of sleep. Because of working from home, they do not neglect their family, partners, but to a certain extent they neglect their friends. The work they do from home fulfils them. They are satisfied with their income and believe in the future of the work they do. They maintain good contacts with other people while working from home and successfully separate their work from home from private life. They do not feel tense and upset while working from home, and they are supported and helped in their work from home by relatives and friends.

When it comes to economic aspects, it is more important for the respondents from BiH who work from home to gain control over their own lives, as well as to spend more time with family members.

For working at home, they believe that the most important thing is a good business idea and the need for a good balance between business and private life. Adequate office space is considered important for successful business from home. Certainly, the most important thing for them is a good balance between business and private life, and earnings come into the background. Adequate dressing for work at home is considered unimportant. They usually turn to friends and family for problems at work, although they do not have major problems at working at home. They believe that a good business plan is the most important thing for the success of future entrepreneurs. Finally, working from home would be recommended as the best option for future entrepreneurs.

When it comes to the freelancers, flexible working hours are the most important thing for the freelancers from BiH, and good earnings for everyone else. Significantly less often than others, they accept freelance as the only source of income. Significantly more often than other freelancers from BiH, they would change their full-time employment for a flexible contract job. Of all the others, developers are significantly more common. They have rarely exercised their right to pension insurance. A huge percentage point out that participation in the "Gig Economy" did not negatively affect their lives. They see the improvement of the position of workers in the "Gig Economy" through the strengthening of trust between workers and employers. The freelancers in BiH believe that the "Gig Economy" can reduce the brain drain abroad.

Montenegro

As in other countries, gender differences have not been determined, and the respondents from Montenegro are on average relatively younger, right after BiH. Unlike in BiH, they are significantly more likely to have high and higher education because it is close to half with a university degree. The type of activity in work from home is mostly trade and education (almost half of the total number). They work from home relatively long.

In many ways, the respondents from Montenegro who work from home are specific. Since they work from home, they have much less time for their activities and hobbies, including engaging in sports and recreational activities, have a shorter and lower quality sleep and pay less attention to family and partner than everyone else, and have slightly less time for friends. However, they are more satisfied with the job than the respondents from Northern Macedonia. They do not differ from others in terms of income satisfaction and assessment of the future success of the work they do. Of all the others, they have a bigger problem to separate their work from home from private life, but they also want social contacts with others less than everyone else while working from home. Because of working from home, they are more tense and upset than everyone else, and relatives and friends are less supportive and helpful with work from home than for most of the respondents from other countries.

The respondents from Montenegro face more problems at work than everyone else, which is why they show inconsistencies in psychosocial behavior, and even confusion. Possible factors may include the nervousness and inconsistency of economic activities, the relatively low level of consumerism, especially at the time of the COVID-19 pandemic. Almost a third are engaged in online trade. In addition to the very unfavorable economic situation, we should not lose sight of the turbulent political context, which has further complicated the otherwise confusing social situation. Although working from home is one of the best choice strategies in such social constellations, the big question is to install the necessary technological infrastructure in a short time, regardless of the fact that the personnel base was probably satisfactory.

Probably the most significant factor of dissatisfaction is the discrepancy between higher education and disincentive jobs, primarily related to online trade, and partly to routine forms of educational content.

When it comes to economic aspects, working from home would be recommended as the best option for employment, although somewhat less than others. When deciding to start a home-based business, they are mostly guided by various savings. Unlike Serbia and Bosnia and Herzegovina, those who work from home in Montenegro try to include their family members to a greater extent. Arranging a working space in the house is not of much importance to them. They emphasize the importance of communication skills and previous experience for good business from home. Unlike home workers in other countries, technical equipment is not particularly important for the success of home work. Further, office space is less expensive than others. More than others, they emphasize the importance of motivation for work. They point out that they usually have no special problems while working from home. If they have fewer problems than others, they seek the help of family members and friends, and they get more by going to professional gatherings and seminars.

When they work as freelancers, the most important thing when choosing a job is their earnings. More than others, they exercised the right to pension insurance, and fewer than others are among those who did not exercise the right to any insurance. Working in the "Gig Economy" did not have a negative impact, neither professionally, nor privately, nor financially. At the same time, the freelancers in Montenegro, less than anyone else, assessed the positive contributions of working in the "Gig Economy" in these areas. They also assessed the contribution of the "Gig Economy" to reducing unemployment and improving the quality of life more negatively than others. They see the improvement of the position of workers in the "Gig Economy" through the improvement of legal regulations. Finally, the freelancers in Montenegro believe that the "Gig Economy" cannot reduce the brain drain abroad.

Northern Macedonia

In addition to the fact that there are no significant differences according to gender, the respondents from Northern Macedonia come immediately after Serbia in terms of average age. According to the level of education, they are second, right after Montenegro with almost a third of those who have a university degree. Like the respondents in Montenegro, they work in a similar percentage in trade and education. According to the length of work from home, they are second, right after Montenegro.

Despite these similarities in the social profile, more differences than similarities with Montenegro were found in psychosocial adjustment. The similarity with the respondents from Montenegro is that due to working from home, they do not have the desired time for sports and recreational activities. It should be especially pointed out that the respondents from Northern Macedonia were the most dissatisfied with the work they currently do from home, although in that respect the differences between the countries do not reach the degree of statistical significance. Probably as a consequence of dissatisfaction with the current job, they are the most skeptical about the perspective of the job they are currently working on in the future. They are significantly less tense and upset about the work they do from home than the respondents from Montenegro. However, after Montenegro, they are still the most tense and upset, and those differences with Serbia reach the level of statistical significance.

The respondents from Northern Macedonia, as well as from Montenegro, are less supported by family, relatives and friends and are more bothered by doing work from home than in Serbia and BiH. It is known that the more educated have a slightly more negative perception of work than home than the less educated. It is difficult to say whether the more educated in Montenegro and Northern Macedonia are more inclined to perceive relatives and friends more negatively in accordance with that, or whether relatives and friends really help them less and bother them more in their work from home.

Respondents from Northern Macedonia differ significantly from those from Montenegro while working from home in that they:

- have more time for various activities and hobbies;
- have somewhat more time to engage in sports—recreational activities;
- have longer and better quality sleep;
- while working from home, they pay more attention to family and friends;
- more successfully separate business from private life;
- they socialize more while doing work from home with other people;
- they are less tense and anxious while doing work from home.

In all of the above, the respondents from Montenegro differ from those from BiH and Serbia.

As we have seen, the respondents from Northern Macedonia are similar to the respondents from Montenegro in some sociodemographic characteristics, and especially in the length of work from home, and partly in the type of activity.

In relation to all the others, they are the most specific in terms of expressed dissatisfaction with the work they currently do from home and pessimistic attitude regarding the maintenance of that work in the future. The main factor in this dissatisfaction seems to be the mismatch between high professional qualifications and low professional demands of home-based jobs, dominated by trade, which is probably not supported and helped enough by relatives and friends because they believe they are capable of greater professional achievements. In that, they are similar to the respondents from Montenegro. Unlike Montenegro, in northern Macedonia there are more protective collectivist patterns than in Montenegro, which is a deeply divided society in various directions. It seems that even from these protective factors, Northern Macedonia is closer to the other two countries than to Montenegro, while Serbia and BiH are more similar to each other than they are similar to Northern Macedonia.

Home-based employees in Northern Macedonia would recommend working from home as the best choice for most. More than BiH and Serbia, they are interested in involving family members in work from home. Like the employees at home in Montenegro, the equipment of the business space in the house for successful work is not important to them. Earnings are the most important indicator of successful work from home, followed by productivity. Adequate appearance in the office is more important to them than others. They point out that working from home is work without working hours, which is why they prefer additional work at home. They find it difficult to lack social communication while working at home. To ensure success in their work, they mostly recommend consultations with experts to future entrepreneurs.

For the freelancers in Northern Macedonia, earnings are the most important thing when choosing a job. They spend significantly more time lecturing from home, except in Serbia, and mostly in research work. They exercised their right to pension insurance significantly more than others. They estimate that working in the "Gig Economy" did not negatively affect their lives in any way.

Serbi

The respondents from Serbia are, on average, the oldest. In terms of educational structure, they are very similar to those from Macedonia, and in terms of higher education to BiH and Northern Macedonia. They have significantly fewer highly educated people who work from home than Montenegro, and more than BiH. They are similar to Montenegro in the length of work from home.

In all previously stated aspects, Serbia is consistently different from Montenegro, and in all others, it is similar to Northern Macedonia, with the fact that they are significantly more satisfied with the work they currently do from home and are more optimistic about the future of that job and have more help and support from friends. Overall, the respondents from Serbia provide the most optimistic picture of working from home and appear to be best psychosocially adapted to that work.

Like everyone else, they think that working from home is the best option for employment. They consider arranging business space important for successful work at home. They believe that previous experience is important for successfully running a home-based business. Earnings are also considered the most important indicator of successful work at home. According to constant work from home they are ambivalent because it is work without working hours. Although they do not have special problems at working at home, when they appear, they solve them with the help of friends and family.

For the freelancers in Serbia, earnings are the most important thing when choosing a job. Significantly less often than other freelancers from Serbia, they would change their full-time job for a flexible contract job. Significantly fewer freelancers from Serbia have health and pension insurance. More than the other, they were not entitled to any insurance. Like everyone else, they are of the opinion that working in the "Gig Economy" did not negatively affect their lives in any way.

DIFFERENCES AND SIMILARITIES

The most significant and numerous differences are between those who work from home in Montenegro and others, especially those in Serbia and BiH. They are the least optimistic about work at home and the "Gig Economy"; they have more psychosocial problems than everyone else, they do not have enough free time for recreational activities, and they also complain about excessive work and the impossibility of separating business from private life. In addition to all that, they are worse than everyone else connected to the primary groups while working from home. Despite this, they believe that informal contacts can contribute the most to a successful home-based business. Moreover, they neglect the importance of better technological equipment for successful work from home. Not only do they evaluate the possibilities of work from home and freelancing worse, but they are often inconsistent and even contradictory. For example, for the successful running of a home-based business, they emphasize the importance of social ties, and try to distance themselves as much as possible from the primary groups and rely primarily on professional development. They emphasize the importance of motivation for a successful home-based business and emphasize a kind of demotivation due to burnout at work and the like. They try to distance themselves from the primary groups during their work, and at the same time they are frustrated by it. Due to all this, the respondents from Montenegro face more problems at work than everyone else, which is why they show inconsistencies in psychosocial behavior, and even confusion. Possible factors may include the nervousness and inconsistency of economic activities, the relatively low level of consumerism, especially at the time of the COVID-19 pandemic. Almost a third are engaged in online trade. In addition to the very unfavorable economic situation, we should not lose sight of the turbulent political context, which has further complicated the otherwise confusing social situation. Although working from home is one of the best choice strategies in such social constellations, the big question is to install the necessary technological infrastructure in a short time, regardless of the fact that the staffing base was probably satisfactory. Probably the most significant factor of dissatisfaction is the discrepancy between higher education and disincentive jobs, primarily related to online trade, and partly to routine forms of educational content.

According to some psychosocial patterns of behavior, the respondents from Northern Macedonia are most similar to them. In terms of the level of education and the type of activity, they are most similar to the respondents from Montenegro. They are also similar in terms of dissatisfaction with the current work from home, especially due to demotivation and routine work given their higher education. Due to the current dissatisfaction, they are not optimistic about working from home or the "Gig Economy." Although they have significantly fewer psychosocial problems due to working from home, they are still more similar in this respect to the respondents from Montenegro than to those from BiH and Serbia. All these aspects of similarities with Montenegro at the same time significantly differentiate them from BiH and Montenegro.

BiH and Serbia are generally the most different from Montenegro and Macedonia. In many respects, they are the opposite of the respondents from Montenegro. Unlike the respondents from Montenegro, they are the youngest, with the lowest education and mostly employed in the IT sector. They have no psychosocial problems; they balance well between business and private life, and they have the support of family and friends at work. They are satisfied with their work and income and maintain good social communication while working from home. They are optimistic about the perspective of their work. They jealously try to preserve all this social and cultural capital, and that is why the most important thing for the success of their work is to preserve the borders between business and private life, for which they need flexible working hours. While for everyone the most important indicator of successful work from home is earnings, it is a good business idea for them, since they are already well positioned financially. They manage to achieve a very harmonious relationship between psychosocial, economic, and cultural patterns while working from home or as freelancers, while among the respondents in Montenegro there are disagreements, contradictions, and even conflicts between these areas.

It is obvious that the respondents from BiH are well adapted to working from home. In our opinion, several factors are important for this adjustment. First, it is about the young population that is highly motivated for work because they are involved in professional life relatively early. Secondly, they are above-average motivated because they are over-proportionally represented in the IT sector. The very fact that their education is below average does not diminish, but probably goes in favor of above-average motivation for the IT sector and programming, because they obviously acquired knowledge and skills in those areas outside the usual institutional framework. In this regard, this population is particularly interesting for monitoring possible directions of development of work from home, partly outside the usual institutional framework, given the strong scepticism that the promotion and development of freelance is possible mainly or only in institutional educational frameworks.

Although the respondents from Serbia have some formal similarities with those from Montenegro (in terms of length of service) and Northern Macedonia (in terms of education), they differ significantly from the respondents from Montenegro in a number of other characteristics, which are more similar to the respondents from BiH. They do not have pronounced psychosocial problems. They are satisfied with their work from home and are optimistic about the future of their work. Like the respondents from BiH, they nurture good social ties for the primary groups and the closer social environment, to which they eventually turn for help due to business problems, which they generally do not have.

Like the others, working from home is considered the best option for employment, and for the success of the business from home, they rely mostly on previous experience. Of the respondents from BiH, they are mostly separated by the belief that earnings are the best indicator of the success of a home-based business. In everything else they are quite similar.

When it comes to similarities, then it is certainly most important that everyone considers working from home the best choice if it is offered to them, and especially when it comes to employment. Truth be told, there is one fence in all; since everyone thinks that working from home has no limits, most would prefer to opt for flexible working hours under contract. Flexible working hours allow everyone greater autonomy in planning and achieving tasks and business goals and open space for personal initiative, freedom, and creativity, which are probably the main reasons why for most working from home there is no alternative. Another common denominator is good earnings. Unfortunately, all of them have in common that workers from home, and especially freelancers, are stepchildren of their countries, because most of them have neither health, nor pension, nor any other insurance. In that respect, the situation with the freelancers in Montenegro is somewhat better, and certainly the worst in Serbia. The most important common denominator is the undivided optimism of almost everyone who works from home, despite numerous difficulties and frustrations in achieving the success of that business, which are more objective than subjective in nature when it comes to the countries of the Western Balkans. Among the objective ones in the first place are limited economic and technological resources for individual entrepreneurial activities (lack or expensive funds to start a business from home, large tax levies and fees, monopolies that restrict and block free market competition, illegal trade channels, corruption, etc.). In such a very unfavorable economic, social, and political environment in the countries of the Western Balkans, working from home, and especially freelancing, remain the only oases of entrepreneurial freedoms and personal autonomy that are not directly affected by these external restrictions. It is a great paradox that this entrepreneurial elite of mostly young people, in which freelancers are at the top or near the top, is positioned by the countries of the Western Balkans on the margins of socioeconomic life.

DISCUSSION AND CONCLUSIONS

In the available literature, we did not find research with a similar research design, neither in terms of the number of countries covered, nor in terms of thematic diversity, so a direct comparison of our main research results is almost impossible. It is possible to compare some more specific phenomena of working from home, which we will do as data from other research becomes available.

By its nature, our research is holistic, which, given the great variety of topics and samples (four countries), has remained at a phenomenological level—describing the impact of economic factors and freelance on various psychosocial aspects of work from home and examining certain functional relationships and differences between these factors.

Due to the lack of empirical base, our research was necessarily exploratory and went broader, while most of the research presented in the literature review covered significantly narrower segments in which explanations of these more specific connections were sought. This is expected given that the experience with different modalities of remote working in developed countries dates back to the 70s of the 20th century. As we have seen from this review, in addition to a large empirical base for remote work research, there is a thorough record on this topic of official statistics in the United Kingdom (OECD, 2014; Germany (Rupietta & Beckman, 2016) Europe, the Netherlands, Matrich, Insight Economic, 2013) United States (Center for Mental Health Statistics, 2020; Center for Disease Control and Prevention, 2020) Japan (Ministry of Health, Labour and Welfare, Japan, 2019) and a number of other countries.

The comparability of the research results, which we stated in the literature review, is difficult at least for several methodological reasons.

The first is the size and representativeness of the samples. The studies that have been done on large samples and that are representative at the national level are rare.

The second is very different methodological approaches. As we have seen, some are based on meta-analysis, others on qualitative data and in-depth interviews, the third on data collected by electronic surveys, and the fourth on data analysis of official health statistics and labor statistics.

The most significant methodological problem, however, is the cognitive scope of these studies. Although in the literature review we have listed a number of brilliant studies that push the boundaries of our knowledge about different aspects of working from home (Burke, 2015; Dockery & Bawa, 2014; Etheridge et al., 2020; Grant et al., 2013; Hay et al., 2020; Mann & Holsworth, 2000; Merecz & Andysz, 2014; Oakman et al., 2020; Rupietta & Beckman, 2016; Song & Gao, 2018; Susilo et al., 2020; Thorstensson, 2020) it is noted that the generalizations of conclusions are limited by the fact that the analysis of results does not include important control variables that can at least relativize the obtained results and conclusions based on them, starting from basic social-demographic variables to more complex social and psychological constructs. This is most often the reason why we get different, even contradictory, findings on the same or similar research problems. Let us just remind ourselves how different the results on job satisfaction, autonomy and productivity are, if, for example, they did not take into account the flexibility of work or the balance between professional and family life, the boundaries between the two and the modalities of their establishment. Things get even more complicated if we do not take gender and age as control variables.

Despite all these limitations, there is a high degree of agreement about certain results that are relevant to our research and that can at least indirectly confirm or call into question our results. However, it should be said that due to all the previously mentioned methodological and other limitations, there are minor or major disagreements about the results on the same or similar topics.

Researchers are almost unanimous about the positive effects of remote working, and significantly less about the negative ones. There is an undivided belief that new information and communication technologies have enabled new forms of remote work, which have contributed to work flexibility and higher productivity, increased autonomy, and freedom and creativity of employees, job satisfaction, significant savings (no lease of office space, reduced utilities and reduced transport costs) greater job satisfaction, reduced sick leave, better communication, job organization and overall business optimization (Allen, 2001; Baltes et al., 1999; Bloom et al., 2015; Galinsky et al., 2008; Gajenndran & Harisson, 2007; Greenhaus & Powell, 2006; Kurland & Baley, 1999; Thomas & Ganster, 1995).

The degree of agreement is influenced by all the previously mentioned methodological limitations and a series of the other for which we would need a lot of time and space to analyze them individually. Certainly, they should result from the interpretation of the results, and that interpretation is primarily under the theoretical inflow from which the researchers start. However, we should not lose sight of the fact that the appropriate ideological matrix influenced the undivided agreement on new modalities of remote work, almost canonized by globalist and neoliberal protagonists. That is why these positive contributions should not be questioned.

The negative aspects of working from home are presented with more nuance and often in a continuum. It is conditioned by all the aforementioned methodological limitations, and sometimes by conscious or less conscious efforts to mitigate the negative consequences. The main catalysts for the negative consequences seem to be two closely related phenomena: working from home for much longer than usual and establishing a balance between work and family. As a rule, much longer work primarily makes it difficult and impossible to establish boundaries between work and family, but this balancing is also influenced by other factors.

As we have said, the balance between work and private life, which primarily refers to the balance between work and family, appears as the relatively most significant difficulty of home employees in our research, while abroad it gets a central place in different contexts (Kreiner et al., 2009; Lewis & Cooper, 2005; Li et al., 2014; Stone, 2012). Recall that in one study, 60% of home employees cited breaking the boundaries between work and private life as a major problem (Ellison, 1999). Therefore, in a number of studies, special attention has been paid to ways of establishing and maintaining boundaries (Ashforth et al., 2000; Clark, 2000; Grant et al., 2013; Nippert-Eng, 1996). Conflicts due to the collapse of borders are the causes or precipitators of a number of symptoms of impaired mental health: stress (Allvin et al., 2011; Demerouti et al., 2014; Dyrbye et al., 2011; Noonnan & Glass, 2012) depression (Holmes et al., 2020) loss of job satisfaction (Hartig et al., 2007) and burnout (Lingard & Francis, 2006).

In one large research of a sample of 1,500 respondents, it was found that the ability to manage working hours was the most important determinant to maintain a work-life balance (Maruyama et al., 2009). It is pointed out that motivation, self-motivation, and self-discipline are key to successful and productive work from home and to achieving the ability to maintain work-life balance (Baruch, 2000; Lupu, 2017; Morgan, 2004; Sullivan & Lewis, 2001). However, this ability to plan jobs and control the execution of plans is difficult to achieve because often the external pressures to work much longer in order to complete tasks are objectively stronger or the employees subjectively perceive them as stronger. According to boundary theory, people use different ways to achieve an optimal level of separation of work from private life (Ashforth et al., 2000; Clark, 2000). Those who have a built-in strategy for border management manage borders more strictly and develop strong segmentation between work and family (Kossek et al., 1999; Nippert-Eng, 1996). Given the previously stated complexity and interdependence of factors that not only help maintain segmentation but also its destruction, we are closer to the idea that greater flexibility of borders is necessary, which means that we view "overflow" as a kind of safety valve when there is a danger of cracking and collapsing borders. Simply maintaining the limits for a longer time only or primarily by voluntary efforts seems risky to us. In the long run, the engagement of volitional capacities becomes counterproductive because the will, which is the basis of harmonious psychological functioning, is a weak mental function.

In the example of the countries of the Western Balkans, this key problem is less present, although it exists. Paradoxically, some patriarchal-collectivist patterns had a positive impact on the marginalization of the problem (somewhat with the exception of Montenegro). We have seen that friends and relatives do not intrude the workspace during the time of those who work from home. In addition, they provide strong emotional and moral support to employees in almost all crisis situations. We said earlier that in Montenegro, these postcollectivist patterns are manifested in a hypertrophied form and affect the collapse of borders. In accordance with the strong collectively narcissistic patterns that permeate the primary groups, including the Montenegrin family, every failure of an individual endangers this idealized family image and results in the denial of family assistance and even rejection. For all these reasons, the sociopsychological profile of home employees contains significantly more negative factors than in the other three countries of the Western Balkans. These examples confirm that similar sociopsychological and cultural patterns can produce significantly different consequences and vice versa.

Despite the fact that respondents from the four Western Balkan countries in a large percentage preferred working from home as the best model of work and recommending it to others, the reverse of this optimistic option exists, which is contained in the relatively often emphasized view that working from home is work without the beginning and the end. This is also a constant that we find in another research (Felstead & Henseke, 2017). In both our and foreign research, remote workers see the best solution in flexible working hours (Ford & Butts, 1991; Wienclaw, 2019). If they manage to develop self-motivation, self-discipline, self-confidence and build appropriate tactics for good planning of daily activities (Baruch, 2000; Morgan, 2004; Richardson & McKenna, 2014; Sullivan & Levis, 2001), working from home becomes a pleasure and raises productivity (Baruch, 2000; Morgan, 2001). If this is not achieved and the employees do not see a way to be excluded from work (Dyrbye et al., 2014; Felstead & Henseke, 2017), almost on the principle of domino effect, numerous disorders and burnout occur (Lingard & Francis, 2006;). As a result of all these problems, there is a poor mental health (Kestrel, 2019; Ministry of Health and Welfare, Japan, 2019; OECD, 2010

In order for remote work to be successful, the necessity of supervision and support of employees is emphasized, training of managers with adequate application of verbal and nonverbal communication with employees (Kowalski & Swanson, 2005). Unfortunately, such trainings are rare or nonexistent (Clear & Dickson, 2005).

In our research, the consequences of the impossibility of being excluded from remote work are relatively milder and are related to the reduction of direct social contacts, and to a lesser extent to monotony, social isolation and sometimes poor sleep. Significantly more pronounced social isolation has been reported in foreign research (Fonner & Roloff, 2012; Pinsonneault & Boisvert, 2001).

The employees in all four countries of the Western Balkans are well psychosocially adapted to the different economic demands of working from home, and even better to accepting the "Gig Economy," which is generally shown by the results of the entire research, analysed in detail earlier. They have a certain ambivalence with remote workers in other countries when it comes to the working status. Although they generally prefer full-time employment, they do not emphasize additional work with flexible working hours. They advocate for flexible working hours for the same reasons as the vast majority of the employees in other countries. However, this discrepancy is predominantly conditioned by very unfavorable factors that are much less pronounced in the Western countries. Although there are some minor differences between the countries of the Western Balkans, all of them have poorly or very poorly regulated their labor rights—the right to health, pension, disability, social insurance. The vast majority do not have any insurance, and the situation is relatively the worst in Serbia. Such a stepmotherly relationship becomes completely incomprehensible if we keep in mind that this is a young, educated population that is mostly employed in the field of information and communication technologies, for the improvement of which all these countries are declaratively committed. Contrary to their wishes and beliefs, remote employees opt for a less risky option. Despite the completely unacceptable measures of the state administration that stifles freelance, Serbia is among the 10 countries in terms of the development of freelance, which speaks of the huge resilience of freelancers in Serbia. Certain ambivalence shown by the employees from home in the four Western Balkan countries is primarily due to the lack of realization of basic labor and social rights when it comes to economic aspects and freelance; while some economic aspects, such as office equipment and clothing, deviate from common standards in other Western countries, conditioned by economic problems, but also by anachronistic patriarchal value patterns.

Finally, this exploratory research, which covers a wide range of topics and issues, showed that the countries of the Western Balkans are a kind of natural laboratory for examining numerous aspects of work from home that do not sufficiently include psychosocial and especially sociocultural factors. A number of differences between our results and the results of foreign researchers can be primarily attributed to psychosocial and sociocultural factors, which in foreign research are either not included or are covered to a lesser extent. As in most similar exploratory research of the holistic type, our research opened more questions than it provided reliable answers.

Such research has one important cognitive function—it expands the epistemological aspects in which directions new research should be designed.

REFERENCES

Aczel, B., Kovacs, M., Van Der Lippe T., & Szaszi, B. (2021). Researchers working from home: Benefits and challenges. *PLoSONE, 16*(3), e0249127. https://doi.org/10.1371/journal.pone.0249127

Adkins, C. L., & Premeaux, S. F. (2012). Spending time: The impact of hours worked on work–family conflict. *Journal of Vocational Behaviour, 80*(2), 380–389.

Allen, T. (2001). Family-supportive Work Environments: The role of organizational perceptions. *Journal of Vocational Behavior, 58*, 414–435.

Allvin, M., Aronsson, G., Hagstrom, T., Johansson, G., & Lundberg, U. (2011). *Work without boundaries: Psychological perspectives on the new working life*. Wiley-Blackwell.

Anderson, A. J., Kaplan, S. A., & Vega, R. P. (2015). The impact of telework on emotional experience: Ehen, and for whom, does telework improve daily affective well-being? *European Journal of Work and Organizational Psychology, 24*(6), 882–897.

Arnfalk, P., Pilerot, U., Schillander, P., & Grönvall, P. (2016). Green IT in practice: Virtual meetings in Swedish public agencies. *Journal of Cleaner Production, 123*, 101–112.

Ashforth, B. E., Kreiner, G. E., & Fugate, M. (2000). All in a day's work: Boundaries and micro role transitions. *Academy of Management Review*, 472–491.

Baert, S., Lippens, L., Moens, E., Weytjens, J., & Sterkens, P. (2020). *The COVID-19 crisis and telework: A research survey on experiences, expectations and hopes* (IZA Discussion Paper No. 13229). Retrieved June 1, 2020, from https://ssrn.com/abstract=3596696

Bailey, D. E., & Kurland, N. B. (2002). A review of telework research: Findings, new directions, and lessons for the study of modern work. *Journal of Organizational Behavior, 23*(4), 383-400.

Bailyn, L. (1988). Freeing work from the constraints of location and time. *New Technology, Work and Employment, 3*(2), 143–152.

Baines, S., & Gelder, U. (2003). What is family friendly about the workplace in the home? The case of self-employed parents and their children. *New Technology, Work and Employment, 18*(3), 223–234.

Bakker, A. B., & Demerouti, E. (2007). The job demands-resources model: State of the art. *Journal of Managerial Psychology, 22*(3), 309–328.

Baltes, B. B., Briggs, T. E., Huff, J. W., Wright, J. A., & Neuman, G. A. (1999). Flexible and compressed workweek schedules: A meta-analysis of their effects on work-related criteria. *Journal of Applied Psychology, 84*, 496–513.

Barnett, R. C., Gareis, K. C., & Brennan, R. T. (1999). Fit as a mediator of the relationship between work hours and burnout. *Journal of Occupational Health Psychology, 4*(4), 307–317. http://dx.doi.org/10.1037/1076- 8998.4.4.307

Baruch, Y. (2000). Teleworking: benefits and pitfalls as perceived by professionals andManagers. *New Technology Work and Employment, 15*(1), 34–49.

Beňo, M. (2018). Working in the virtual world—An approach to the "Home Office" business model analysis. *Journal of Interdisciplinary Research, 8*(1), 25–36.

Bentley, T., Teo, S., McLeod, L., Tan, F., Bosua, R., & Gloet, M. (2016). The role of organisational support in teleworker wellbeing: A socio-technical systems approach. *Applied Ergonomics, 52*, 207–215.

Binder M., & Coad A. (2016). How satisfied are the self-employed? A life domain view. *Journal of Happiness Studies, 17*(4), 1409–1433.

Bouziri, H., Smith, D. R., Descatha, A., Dab, W., & Jean, K. (2020). Working from home in the time of COVID-19: How to best preserve occupational health? *Occupational and Environmental Medicine, 77*, 509–510.

Brynjolfsson, E., Horton, J. J., Ozimek, A., Rock, D., Sharma, G., & TuYe, H.-Y. (2020). *COVID-19 and remote work: An early look at US data* (Working Paper Series, No. 27344). National Bureau of Economic Research.

Bhat, S. K., Pande, N., & Ahuja, V. (2017). Virtual team effectiveness: An empirical study using SEM. *Procedia Computer Science, 122*, 33–41.

Beckers, D. G., Kompier, M. A., Kecklund, G., & Härmä, M. (2012). Worktime control: Theoretical conceptualization, current empirical knowledge, and research agenda. *Scandinavian Journal of Work, Environment & Health, 38*, 291–297.

Bloom, N., Liang, J., Roberts, J., & Ying, Z. J. (2015). Does working from home work? Evidence from a Chinese experiment. *Quarterly Journal of Economics, 130*(1), 165–218.

Bolger, N., DeLongis, A., Kessler, R. C., & Wethington, E. (1989). The contagion of stress across multiple roles. *Journal of Marriage and the Family, 51*(1), 175–183. https://doi.org/10.2307/352378

Bosua, R., Gloet, M., Kurnia, S., Mendoza, A., & Yong, J. (2013). Telework, productivity and wellbeing: An Australian perspective. *Telecommunications Journal of Australia. 63*(1), 11.1–11.12.

Burke, A. (2015). *The handbook of research on freelancing and self-employment.* Senate Hall Academic.

Carlson, D. S., Grzywacz, J. G., & Kacmar, K. M. (2010). The relationship of schedule flexibility and outcomes via the work-family interface. *Journal of Managerial Psychology, 25*(4), 330–355.

Cassells, R., Gong, H., & Duncan, A. (2011, November). Race against time: How Australians spend their time. *AMP.NATSEM Income and Wealth Report, 30.*

Centers for Disease Control and Prevention. (2020). *Symptoms of coronavirus—Coronavirus Disease 2019 (COVID-19).* Retrieved May 2020, from cdc.gov: https://www.cdc.gov/coronavirus/2019-ncov/symptoms-testing/symptoms.html

Center for National Health Statistics. (2020, June). *Mental health: Household Pulse Survey.* Retrieved June 17, 2020, from cdc.gov: https://www.cdc.gov/nchs/covid19/pulse/mental-health.htm

Cho, E., Tay, L., Allen, T. D., & Stark, S. (2013). Identification of a dispositional tendency to experience work-family spillover. *Journal of Vocational Behaviour, 82*(3), 188–198, http://dx.doi.org/10.1016/ j.jvb.2013.01.006

Clark, S. C. (2000). Work/family border theory: A new theory of work/family balance. *Human Relations, 53*(6), 47–70.

Clear, F., & Dickson, K. (2005). Teleworking practice in small and medium-sized firms: management style and worker autonomy. *New Technology, Work and Employment, 20*(3), 218–232.

Cogliser, C. C., Gardner, W. L., Gavin, M. B., & Broberg, J. C. (2012). Big five personality factors and leader emergence in virtual teams: Relationships with team trustworthiness, member performance contributions, and team performance. *Group & Organisation Management 37*(6), 752–784.

Cooper, C. D., & Kurland, N. B. (2002). Telecommuting, professional isolation, and employee development in public and private organizations. *Journal of Organizational Behavior, 23*(4), 511–532.

Čulo, K. (2016). Virtual organization—The future has already begun. *Media Culture and Public Relations, 7,* 35–42.

Daim, T. U., Ha, A., Reutiman, S., Hughes, B., Pathak, U., Bynum, W., & Bhatla, A. (2012). Exploring the communication breakdown in global virtual teams. *International Journal of Project. Management, 30,* 199–212.

Daverth, G., Hyde, P., & Cassell, C. (2016). Uptake of organisational work-life balance opportunities: The context of support. *International Journal of Human Resource Management, 27*(15), 1710–1729.

De Bloom, J., Sianoja, M., Korpela, K., Tuomisto, M., Lilja, A., Geurts, S., & Kinnunen, U. (2017). Effects of park walks and relaxation exercises during lunch breaks on recovery from job stress: Two randomized controlled trials. *Journal of Environmental Psychology, 51,* 14–30.

Demerouti, E., Derks, D., Brummelhuis, L. L. T., & Bakker, A. B. (2014). New ways of working: Impact on working conditions, work-family balance, and well-being, In C. Korunka & P. Hoonakker (Eds.), *The impact of ICT on quality of working life* (pp. 123–141), Springer Science and Business Media.

Dockery, A. M., & Bawa, S. (2014). Is working from home good work or bad work? Evidence from Australian employees. *Australian Journal of Labour, 17*(2), 163–190.

DuBrin, A. J. (1991). Comparison of the job satisfaction and productivity of telecommuters versus in-house employees: A research note on work in progress. *Psychological Reports, 68*(3c), 1223–1234.

Dutcher, E. G. (2012). The effects of telecommuting on productivity: An experimental examination. The role of dull and creative tasks. *Journal of Economic Behavior and Organization, 84*(1), 355–363.

Duxbury, L., Stevenson, M., & Higgins, C. (2018). Too much to do, too little time: Role overload and stress in a multi-role environment. *International Journal of Stress Management, 25*(3), 250–266. https://doi.org/10.1037/str0000062

Dyrbye, L. N., Shanafelt, T. D., Balch, C. M., Satele, D., Sloan, J., & Freischlag, J. (2011). Relationship between work-home conflicts and burnout among American surgeons: A comparison by sex. *Archives of Surgery, 146*(2), 211–217, http://dx.doi.org/10.1001/archsurg.2010.310

Eddleston, K. A., & Mulki, J. (2017). Toward understanding remote workers' management of work-family boundaries: the complexity of workplace embeddedness. *Group and Organizational Management, 42*(3), 346–387.

Eikhof, D. R., Warhurst, C., & Haunschild, A. (2007). What work? What life? What balance? Critical reflections on the work-life balance debate. *Employee Relations, 29*(4), 325–333.

Elison, N. B. (1999). Social impacts: New perspectives on tele-work. *Social Science Computer Review, 17*(3), 338–356.

Etheridge, B., Wang, B., & Tang, L. (2020). *Worker productivity during lockdown and working from home: Evidence from self-reports* (ISER Working Paper Series 2020-12). Institute for Social and Economic Research.

Fan, W., Lam, J., & Moen, P. (2019). Stress proliferation? Precarity and work-family conflict at the intersection of gender and household income. *Journal of Family Issues, 40*(18), 2751–2773. https://doi.org/10.1177/0192513X19862847

Felstead A., & Henseke G. (2017). Assessing the growth of remote working and its consequences for effort, well-being and work-life balance. *New Technology, Work and Employment, 32*(3), 195–212.

Fiksenbaum, L., Koyuncu, M., & Burke, R. J. (2010). Virtues, work experiences and psychological well-being among managerial women in a Turkish bank. *Equality, Diversity and Inclusion, 29*(2), 199–212. http://dx.doi.org/10.1108/02610151011024501

Fílardí F., de Castro, R., & Zaníní, M. T. F. (2020). Advantages and disadvantages of teleworking in Brazilian public administration: Analysis of SERPRO and Federal Revenue experiences. *Cadernos EBAPE.BR, 18*(1), 28–46.

Flesia, L., Fietta, V., Colicino, E., Segatto, B., & Monaro, M. (2020, May 5). *Stable psychological traits predict perceived stress related to the COVID-19 outbreak.* https://psyarxiv.com:https://psyarxiv.com/yb2h8/download/?format=pdf

Flüter-Hoffmann, C. (2012). Erfolgsgeschichte Telearbeit – Arbeitsmodell der Zukunft [Success story telework—working model of the future]. In B. Badura, A. Ducki, H. Schröder, J. Klose, & M. Meyer (Eds.), *Fehlzeiten-Report. Gesundheit in der flexiblen Arbeitswelt: Chancen nutzen – Risiken minimieren* (pp. 71–77). Zahlen, Daten, Analysen aus allen Branchen der Wirtschaft. Springer.

Fonner, K. L., & Roloff, M. E. (2012, June 1). Testing the connectivity paradox: Linking teleworkers' communication media use to social presence, stress from interruptions, and organizational identification. *Communication Monographs, 79*(2), 205–231.

Ford, R. C., & Butts, M. A. (1991). Is your organization ready for telecommuting? *SAM Advanced Management Journal, 56*(4), 19+. https://link.gale.com/apps/doc/A12106285/AONE?u=anon~fc76df19&sid=googleScholar&xid=f8bd2661

Gajendran, R. S., & Harrison, D. A. (2007). The good, the bad, and the unknown about telecommuting: Meta-analysis of psychological mediators and individual consequences. *Journal of Applied Psychology, 92*(6), 1524–1541.

Galinsky, E., Bond, J., & Sakai, K. (2008), 2008 National Study of Employers. Retrieved January 28, 2009, from http://familiesandwork.org/site/research/reports/2008nse.pdf

Gimenez-Nadal, J. I., Molina, J. A., & Velilla, J.(2020). Work time and well-being for workers at home: Evidence from the American time use survey. *International Journal of Manpower, 41*(2), 184–206.

Golden, T. D. (2012). Altering the effects of work and family conflict on exhaustion: Telework during traditional and nontraditional work hours. *Journal of Business and Psychology, 27*(3), 255–269.

Graham, M., Lehdonvirta, V., Wood, A., Barnard, H., Hjorth, I., & Simon, D. P. (2017). *The risks and rewards of online gig work at the global margins.* Oxford Internet Institute.

Grant, C. A., Wallace, L. M., & Spurgeon. P. C. (2013). An exploration of the psychological factors affecting worker's job effectiveness, well-being and worklife balance. *Employee Relations, 35*(5), 527–546.

Gray, J. A. & Muramatsu, N. (2011). Work Stress, burnout, and social and personal resources among direct care workers. *Research in developmental disabilities, 32*,106574. https://doi.org/10.1016/j.ridd.2011.01.025

Greenhaus, J. H., & Powell, G. N. (2006). When work and family are allies: a theory of work–family enrichment. *Academy of Management Review, 31,* 72–92.

Großer, B., & Baumöl, U. (2017). Why virtual teams work—State of the art. *Procedia Computer Science, 121,* 297–305.

Grzywacz, J. G. (2000). Work-family spillover and health during midlife: Is managing conflict everything? *American Journal of Health Promotion, 14*(4), 236–243, http://dx.doi.org/10.4278/0890-1171-14.4.236

Grzywacz, J. G., & Bass, B. L. (2003). Work, family, and mental health: Testing different models of work family fit. *Journal of Marriage and Family, 65*(1), 248–261. http://dx.doi.org/10.1111/j.1741-3737.2003.00248.x

Gurstein, P. (1996). Planning for telework and home-based employment: Reconsidering the home/work separation. *Journal of Planning Education and Research, 15*(3), 212–224.

Hackman, J. R., & Oldham, G. R. (1976). Motivation through the design of work: Test of a theory. *Organizational Behavior and Human Performance, 16*(2), 250-279.

Haddon, L., & Lewis, A. (1994). The experience of teleworking: An annotated review. *International Journal of Human Resource Management, 5*(1), 193–223.

Halford, S. (2005). Hybrid workspace: Re-spatialisations of work, organisation and management. *New Technology Work and Employment, 20,* 19–33.

Hall, D. (1972). A model of coping with role conflict: The role behaviour of college educated women. *Administrative Science Quarterly, 17*(4), 471–486.

Hall, D. T., & Richter, J. (1988). Balancing work life and home life: What can organizations do to help? *The Academy of Management Executive, 2*(3), 213–23. http://dx.doi.org/10.5465/AME.1988.4277258.

Hartig, T., Kylin, C., & Johansson, G. (2007). The telework trade off: Stress mitigation vs constrained restoration. *Applied Psychology: An International Review, 56*(2), 23.

Hayes, S., Priestley, J. L., Ishmakhametov, N., & Ray, H. E. (2020). *I'm not working from home, i'm living at work: Perceived stress and work-related burnout before and during COVID-19.* PsyArXivs Preprints. https://psyarxiv.com/vnkwa/

Hayman, J. (2010). Flexible work schedules and employee well-being. *New Zealand Journal of Employment Relations, 35*(2), 76–87.

Henke, R. M., Benevent, R., Schulte, P., Rinehart, C., Crighton. K., & Corcoran, M. (2016). The effects of telecommuting intensity on employee health. *American Journal of Health Promotion, 30*(8), 604–612.

Hill, E. J., Ferris, M., & Märtinson, V. (2003). "Does it matter where you work? A comparison of how three work venues (traditional office, virtual office, and home office) influence aspects of work and personal/family life. *Journal of Vocational Behaviour, 63*(2), 220–241.

Hobfoll, S. E. (2001). The influence of culture, community, and the nested-self in the stress process: Advancing conservation of resources theory. *Applied Psychology, 50*(3), 337–421. http://dx.doi.org/10.1111/1464-0597.00062

Holmes, E. A., O'Connor, R. C., Perry, V. H., Tracey, I., Wessely, S., Arseneault, L., Ballard, C., Christensen, H., Cohen Silver, R., Everall, I., Ford, A., Kabir, T., K., King, Madan, I., Michie, S., Przybylski , A. K., Shafran, R., Sweeney A., Sweeney, C. M., Worthman, Yardley, L., Cowan, K., Cope, C., Hotopf, M., & Bullmore, E. (2020). Multidisciplinary research priorities for the COVID-19 pandemic: A call for action for mental health science. *The Lancet Psychiatry, 7*(6), 547–560.

Hornung, S., & Glaser, J. (2009). Home-based telecommuting and quality of life: further evidence on an employee-oriented human resource practice. *Psychological Reports, 104*(2), 395–402.

Huws, U. (1984). *The new homeworkers: New technology and the changing location of white-collar work* (Low Pay Pamphlet, No. 28). Low Pay Unit.

Jackman, S. (2019, November 5). Microsoft japan says four-day work week boosted productivity 40%. *Bloomberg.* Retrieved April 14, 2020, from https://www.bloomberg.com/news/articles/2019-11-04/microsoft-japan-says-fourdaywork-week-boosted-productivity-40

Jensen, G. (1994). *Balancing the work/home interface: Challenge and solutions.* Utah State University.

Johnson, J. V., & Hall, E. M. (1988). Job strain, work place social support, and cardiovascular disease: A cross sectional study of a random sample of the Swedish working population. *American Journal of Public Health, 78*(10), 1336–1342, http://dx.doi.org/10.2105/ AJPH.78.10.1336

Kaduk, A., Genadek, K., Kelly. E. L., & Moen P. (2019). Involuntary vs. voluntary flexible work: Insights for scholars and stakeholders. *Community Work and Family, 22*(4), 412–442.

Karkoulian, S., Srour, J., & Sinan, T. (2016). A gender perspective on work-life balance, perceived stress, and locus of control. *Journal of Business Research*, *69*(11), 4918–4923. https://doi.org/10.1016/j.jbusres.2016.04.053

Kazekami, S. (2020). Mechanisms to improve labor productivity by performing telework. *Telecommunications Policy*, *44*(2), 101868.

Keene, J. R., & Quadagno, J. (2004). Predictors of perceived work-family balance: Gender difference or gender similarity? *Sociological Perspectives*, *47*(1), 1–23. http://dx.doi.org/10.1525/ sop.2004.47.1.1

Keeton, K., Fenner, D. E., Johnson, T. R. B., & Hayward, R. A. (2007). Predictors of physician career satisfaction, work-life balance, and burnout. *Obstetrics & Gynecology*, *109*(4), 949.

Kestrel, D. (2019). *Mental health in the workplace*. World Health Organization. Retrieved August 19, 2019, from https://www.who.int/news-room/commentaries/detail/ mental-health-in-the-workplace

Kim, S., & Hollensbe, E. (2017, Jan. 1). Work interrupted: A closer look at work boundary permeability. *Management Research Review*, *40*(12), 1280–1297.

Kossek, E. E., & Lautsch, B. A. (2018). Work-life flexibility for whom? Occupational status and work–life inequality in upper, middle, and lower level jobs. *Academy of Management Annals*, *12*(1), 5–36.

Kossek, E. E., Noe, R., & DeMarr, B. J. (1999). Work-family role synthesis: Individual and organizational determinants. *International Journal of Conflict Management*, *10*(2), 102–129.

Kotera, Y., Green, P., & Shefield, D. (2018). Work-life balance of UK construction workers: Relationship with mental health. *Construction Management and Economics*, *38*, 291–303.

Kowalski, B. K., & Swanson, J. A. (2005). Critical success factors in developing teleworking Programs. *Benchmarking: An international Journal*, *12*(3), 236–249.

Krahn, H. (1995, Winter). Non-standard work on the rise. *Perspectives on Labour and Income*, *7*, 35–42.

Kreiner G. E., Hollensbe E. C., & Sheep M. L. (2009). Balancing borders and bridges: Negotiating the work-home interface via boundary work tactics. *Academy of Management Journal*, *52*(4), 704–730.

Kristensen, T., Borritz, M., Villadsen, E., & Christensen, K. (2005). The Copenhagen Burnout Inventory: A new tool for the assessment of burnout. *Work & Stress*, *19*(3), 192–207. https://doi.org/10.1080/02678370500297720

Kurland, N. B., & Bailey, D. E. (1999). The advantages and challenges of working here, there, anywhere, and anytime. *Organisational Dynamics*, *28*(2), 53–68.

Kuscu, M., & Hasan, A. (2016). Virtual leadership at distance education teams. *Turkish Online Journal Distance Education*, *17*, 136–156.

Langballe, E. M., Innstrand, S. T., Aasland, O. G., & Falkum E. (2011). The predictive value of individual factors, work-related factors, and work-home interaction on burnout in female and male physicians: A longitudinal study. *Stress Health*, *27*(1), 73–87. http://dx.doi.org/10.1002/smi.1321

Lavelle, J. (2020, April 3). *Gartner CFO Survey reveals 74% intend to shift some employees to remote work permanently.* Retrieved July 2020, from gartner.com: https://www.gartner.com/en/newsroom/press-releases/2020-04-03-gartner-cfo-survey-reveals-74-percent-of-orgs-to-shift-some-employees-to-remote-work-permanently

LeanIn.org and Survey Monkey. (2020, May 7). *Women are maxing out—and burning out—during COVID-19.* Retrieved June 1, 2020, fromleanin.org:https://media.sgff.io/sgff_r1eHetbDYb/2020-05-07/1588873077242/women-armaxing-outduring-covid-19_1.pdf

Lewis, S., & Cooper, C. L. (2005). *Work-life integration.* Wiley.

Lewis, R., Ferragamo, C., & Yarker, J. (2020). *The psychological impact of remote rotational work.* Internationas FOS Fondation. Afinity Health at Work.

Li, J., Johnson, S., Han, W., Andrews, S., Strazdins, L., Kendall, G., & Dockery, A. (2014), Parents' non-standard work schedules and child wellbeing. A critical review of the literature. *Journal of Primary Prevention, 35*(1), 53–,73.

Lim, V., & Kim, T. (2014). The long arm of the job: Parents' work–family conflict and youths' work centrality. *Applied Psychology: An International Review. 63*(1), 151–167. https://doi.org/10.1111/j.1464-0597.2012.00527.x

Lingard, H., & Francis, V. (2006). Does a supportive work environment moderate the relationship between work-family conflict and burnout among construction professionals? *Construction Management and Economics, 24*(2), 185–96. https://doi.org/10.1080/14697010500226913

Lupu, V. L. (2017). Teleworking and its benefits on work-life balance. *International Multidisciplinary Scientific Conference on Social Sciences & Arts SGEM,* 693.

Madsen, S. R. (2011). The benefits, challenges, and implication of teleworking: A literature review. *Journal of Culture and Religion, 1*(1), 148– 158.

Major, D. A., Verive, J. M., & Joice, W. (2008). Telework as a dependent care solution: examining current practice to improve telework management strategies. *The Psychologist-Manager Journal, 11*(1), 65–91.

Mann, S., & Holdsworth, L. (2000). The psychological impact of teleworking: stress, emotions and health. *New Tehnology, Work and Employment, 18*(3), 196–211.

Mann, S., Varey, S., & Button, W. (2000). An Exploration of the emotional impact of televorking. *Journal of Managerial Psychology, 15*(7), 668–690.

Maruyama, T., Hopkinson, P. G., & James, P. W. (2009). A multivariate analysis of work-life balance outcomes from a large-scale telework programme. *New Technology, Work and Employment, 24*(1), 76–88.

Maslach, C. (1982). *Burnout: The cost of caring.* Prentice-Hall.

Maslach, C., & Leiter, M. P. (2016). Understanding the burnout experience: Recent research and its implications for psychiatry. *World Psychiatry: Official Journal of the World Psychiatric Association (WPA), 15*(2), 103–111. https://doi.org/10.1002/wps.20311

Maslach, C., Schaufeli, W. B., & Leiter, M. P. (2001). Job burnout. *Annual Review of Psychology, 52*(1), 397–422, http://dx.doi.org/10.1146/ annurev.psych.52.1.397.

Matrix Insight Economic. (2013). *Analysis of workplace mental health promotion and mental disorder prevention programmes.* Executive Agency for Health and Consumers.

Mazmanian, M., Orlikowski, W. J., & Yates, J. (2013). The autonomy paradox: The implications of mobile email devices for knowledge professionals. *Organization Science*, *24*, 1337–1357.

Merecz, D., & Andysz, A. (2014). Burnout and demographic characreistics of experiencing different types of work-home interaction. *International Journal of Occupational Medicine and Environmental Health*, *27*(6), 933–949 http://dx.doi.org/10.2478/s13382-014-0320-6

Ministry of Health, Labour and Welfare, Japan. (2019). *White Paper for Prevention for Karoushi etc*. [Karoushi nado boushitaisaku hakusho].

Montreuil, S., & Lippel, K. (2003). Telework and occupational health: A Quebec empirical study and regulatory implications. *Safety Science*, *41*(4), 339–335.

Morgan, R. E. (2004). Teleworking: an assessment of the benefits and challenges. *European Business Review*, *16*(4), 344–357.

Nijp, H. H., Beckers, D. G. J., Van De Voorde, K., Geurts, S. A. E., & Kompier, M. A. J. (2016). Effects of new ways of working on work hours and work location, health and job-related outcomes. *Chronobiology International*, *33*(6), 604–618.

Nippert-Eng C. (1996). Calendars and keys: The classification of "home" and "work". *Sociological Forum*, *11*(3), 563–582.

Noonan, M. C., & Glass, J. (2012). The hard truth about telecommuting. *Monthly Labor Review*, *135*(6), 38–45.

Oakman, J., Kinsman, N., Stuckey, R., Graham, M., & Weale, V. (2020). A rapid review of mental and physical health effects of working at home: How dowe optimise health? *BMC Public Health*, *20*, 1825. https://doi.org/10.1186/s12889-020-09875-z

Organization for Economic Cooperation and Development. (2014). *Mental health and work*.

Olson, M. H. (1989). Work at home for computer professionals: Current attitudes and future prospects. *ACM Transactions on Information Systems (TOIS)*, *7*(4), 317–338.

Ospina, S. (2017). Collective leadership and context in public administration: Bridging public leadership research and leadership studies. *Public Administration Review*, *77*, 275–287.

Pekrun, R., & Frese, M. (1992). Emotions in work and achievement. *International Review of Industrial and Organizational Psychology*, *7*, 153–200.

Peeters, M. C. W., Montgomery, A. J., Bakker, A. B., & Schaufeli, W. B. (2005). Balancing work and home: How job and home demands are related to burnout. *Journal of Stress Management*, *12*(1), 43–61. http://dx.doi.org/10.1037/1072-5245.12.1.43

Petterson, S., Westfall, J., & Miller, B. (2020, May 8). *Projected deaths of despair during the coronavirus recession*. Retrieved June 17, 2020, from WellBeing Trust: https://wellbeingtrust.org/wpcontent/uploads/2020/05/WBT_Deaths-of-Despair_COVID-19-FINAL-FINAL.pdf

Pinsonneault, A., & Boisvert, M. (2001). The impacts of telecommuting on organizations and individuals: A review of the literature. In N. J. Johnson (Ed.), *Telecommuting and virtual offices: Issues and opportunities* (pp. 163–85). IGI Global.

Premeaux, S. F., Adkins, C. L., & Mossholder, K. W. (2007). Balancing work and family: A field study of multi-dimensional, multi-role work-family conflict. *Journal of Organisational Behaviour, 28*(6), 705–727.

Pritchard, R. D., & Payne, S. C. (2003). Performance management practices and motivation. In D. Holman, T. D. Wall, C. W. Clegg, P. Sparrow, & A. Howard (Eds.), *The new workplace: A guide to the human impact of modern working practices* (pp. 219–244). Wiley & Sons.

Proost, K., de Witte, H., de Witte, K., & Evers G. (2004). Burnout among nurses: Extending the job demand-control-support model with work-home interference. *Psychologica Belgica, 44*(4), 269–290. http://dx.doi.org/10.5334/pp

Raghuram, S., Hill, S., Gibbs, J., & Maruping, L. (2019). Virtual work: bridging research clusters. *Academy of Management Annals, 13*(1), 308–341.

Reuschke D. (2019). The subjective well-being of homeworkers across life domains. *Environment and Planning A: Economy and Space, 51*(6), 1326–1349.

Richardson, J., & McKenna S. (2014). Reordering spatial and social relations: A case study of professional and managerial flexworkers. *British Journal of Management, 25*(4), 724–741.

Rigotti, T., De Cuyper, N., & Sekiguchi, T. (2020). The corona crisis: What can we learn from earlier studies in applied psychology? *Applied Psychology: An International Review, 69*(3), 1–6. https://doi.org/10.1111/apps.12265

Rook, K. S. (1984). Research on social support loneliness, and social isolation: Toward an integration. In P. Shaver (Ed.), *Review of personality and social psychology: Emotions, relationship and health*. SAGE.

Rothbard, N. P., Phillips, K. W., Dumas, T. L. (2005). Managing multiple roles: Work-family policies and individuals' desires for segmentation. *Organization Science, 16*(3), 243–258. http://dx.doi. org/10.1287/orsc.1050.0124

Rupietta, K., & Beckman, M. (2016). *Working from home: What is the effect on employees' effort?* (Working papers, 2016/07). Faculty of Business and Economics–University of Basel.

Sandford, A. (2020, April 3). *Coronavirus: Half of humanity now on lockdown as 90 countries call for confinement*. Retrieved May 18, 2020, from euronews.cohttps://www.euronews.com/2020/04/02/coronavirus-in-europe-spain-s-death-toll-hits-10-000-after-record-950-new-deaths-in-24-hour

Sardeshmukh, S. R., Sharma, D., & Golden, T. D. (2012). Impact of telework on exhaustion and job engagement: A job demands and job resources model. *New Technology Work and Employment, 27*(3), 193–207.

Secon, H., & Woodward, A. (2020, March 27). *A map of the US cities and states under lockdown—and those that are reopening*. https://www.businessinsider.com/us-map-stay-at-home-orders-lockdowns-2020-3

Shirom, A., Nirel, N., & Vinokur, A. (2010). Work hours and caseload as predictors of physician burnout: The mediating effects by perceived workload and by autonomy. *Applied Psychology: An International Review, 59*(4), 539–565. https://doi.org/10.1111/j.1464-0597.2009.00411.x

Salanova, M., & Lorens, S. (2008). Current state of research on burnout and future challenges. *Papeles de Psicólogo, 29*(1), 59–67.

Snellman, C. L. (2014). Virtual teams: Opportunities and challenges for e-Leaders. *Procedia—Social and Behavioral Sciences, 110*, 1251–1261.

Song, Y., & Gao, J. (2020). Does telework stress employees out? A study on working at home and subjective well-being for wage/salary workers. *Journal of Happiness Studies, 21*, 2649–2668.

Stachova, K., Stacho, Z. ,Blstakova, J. ,Hlatká, M., & Kapustina, L. M. (2018). Motivation of employees for creativity as a form of support to manage innovation processes in transportation-logistics companies. *Naše More, 65*, 180–186.

Stamper, C. L., & Johlke, M. C. (2003). The impact of perceived organizational support on the relationship between boundary spanner role stress and work outcomes. *Journal of Management, 29*(4), 569–588. https://doi.org/10.1016/S0149-2063_03_00025-4

Steenbergen, V. E., Van der Ven, C., Peeters, M. C. W., & Taris, T. W. (2018). Transitioning towards new ways of working: Do job demands, job resources, burnout, and engagement change? *Psychological Reports, 121*, 736–766.

Stone, K. W. (2012) The decline in the standard employment contract: Evidence from ten advanced industrial countries (2012). K. V. W. Stone & H. Arthurs (Eds.), *After the standard contract of employment: Innovations for regulatory design*. Russell Sage Foundation Press.

Suh, A., & Lee, J. (2017). Understanding teleworkers' technostress and its influence on job satisfaction. *Internet Research, 27*(1), 140–159.

Sullivan, C. (2012). Remote working and work-life balance. In P. Nora, M. J. Sirgy, C. A. Gorman (Eds), *Work and quality of life* (pp. 275–290). Springer.

Sullivan, C., & Lewis, S. (2001). Home-based telework, gender, and the synchronization of work and family: perspectives of teleworkers and their co-residents. *Gender Work and Organization, 8*(2), 123–145.

Susilo, A., Rumende, C. M., Pitoyo, C. W., Santoso, W. D., Yulianti, M., Herikurniawan, H., Sinto, R., Singh, G., Nainggolan, L., Nelwan, E. J., Chen, L. K., Widhani, A., Wijaya, E., Wicaksana, B., Maksum, M., Annisa, F., Jasirwan, C. O. M., & Yunihastuti, E. (2020). Coronavirus disease 2019: Review of current literatures. *Jurnal Panuakit Dalam Indonesia, 7*(1), 45–67.

Taylor, M. K. (2018). Xennials: A microgeneration in the workplace. *Industrial Commercial Training, 50*, 136–147.

Thomas, L. T., & Ganster, D. C. (1995). Impact of family-supportive work variables on work-family conflict and strain: A control perspective. *Journal of Applied Psychology, 80*, 6–15.

Thorstensson, E. (2020). *The influence of working from home on employees' productivity comparative document analysis between the years 2000 and 2019–2020.* Digitala Vetenskapliga Arkivet. http://www.diva-portal.org/smash/record.jsf?pid=diva2%3A1446903&dswid=9368

Turner, J. (1998, July). Will telecommuting ever get off the ground? *The Cincinnati Enquirer, 19.*

Twentyman, J. (2010, September 21). The flexible workforce. *The Times*, pp. 1–16.

Vander, E. T., Verhoogen, R., Sercu, M., Van den Broeck, A., Baillien, E., & Godderis, L. (2017). Not extent of telecommuting, but job characteristics as proximal predictors of work-related well-being. *Journal of Occupational and Environmental Medicine, 59*(10), 1.

Verburg, R., Bosch-Sijtsema, P., & Vartiainen, M. (2013). Getting it done: Critical success factors for project managers in virtual work settings. *International Journal of Project. Management*, *31*, 67–79.

Vilhelmson B., & Thulin E. (2016). Who and where are the flexible workers? Exploring the current diffusion of telework in Sweden. *New Technol Work Employ*, *31*(1), 77–96.

Vischer, J. C. (2007). The effects of the physical environment on job performance: Towards a theoretical model of workspace stress. *Stress and health: Journal of the International Society for the Investigation of Stress*, *23*(3), 175–184. https://doi.org/10.1002/smi.1134

Weinert, C., Maier, C., & Laumer, S. (2015) Why are teleworkers stressed? An empirical analysis of the causes of telework-enabled stress. *Wirtschaftsinformatik Proceedings 2015*, 94. https://aisel.aisnet.org/wi2015/94

Wienclaw, R. A. (2019). Telecommuting. *Salem Press Encyclopedia*. Retrieved May 2, 2020, from https://search.ebscohost.com/login.aspx?direct=true&db=ers&AN=89185784&lang=sv&site= eds-live

Williams, P., Pocock, B., & Skinner, N. (2008). Clawing back time: Expansive working time and implications for work-life outcomes in Australian workers. *Employment & Society*, *22*(4), 737–748.

Wheatley, D. (2012). Good to be home? Time use and satisfaction levels among home-based teleworkers. *New Technology, Work & Employment*, *27*(3), 224–241.

Wheatley, D. (2017). Employee satisfaction and use of flexible working arrangements. *Work, Employment and Society*, *31*(4), 567–585.

Wood, B. A., Guimaraes, A. B., Holm, C. E., Hayes, S. W., & Brooks, K. R. (2020). Academic librarian burnout: A survey using the copenhagen burnout inventory (CBI). *Journal of Library Administration*, *60*(5), 512–531. https://doi.org/10.1080/01930826.2020.1729622

Wooden, M., Warren, D., & Drago, R. (2009). Working time mismatch and subjective wellbeing. *British Journal of Industrial Relations*, *47*(1), 147–179.

APPENDIX I

Questionnaire for the Economic Part: Doing Business From Home by Countries (Montenegro, B&H, Serbia, and North Macedonia)

- Gender:
a. Male
b. Female

- Age:
a. 18–25
b. 26–34
c. 35–44
d. 45–54
e. 55–64
    - Country: _____
    - Education:
        a. Primary school
        b. Secondary school
        c. High school (vocational)
        c. University
- How long have you been working from home?
a. 1 to 5 years

Macroeconomics of Western Balkans in the Context of the Global Work and Business Environment, pp. 155–159
Copyright © 2022 by Information Age Publishing
www.infoagepub.com
155

    b. 6 to 10 years
    c. 11 to 15 years
    d. More than 15 years
- In what activity do you work from home?
  - a. Industry
  - b. Trade
  - c. Tourism
  - d. Construction
  - e. Transportation
  - f. Education
  - **g. Other**

1. Would you recommend this way of working to others as the best choice for employment?
   - a. Yes
   - b. No
   - c. Maybe
   - d. In case it is the only choice for employment

2. I do not know the benefits of doing business from home
   - a. Spending more time with family
   - b. The risk of starting a business is reduced
   - c. The business is gradually developing with the support of the family
   - d. Additional income is provided for family
   - e. Full control over one's life is established
   - **f. Other:**

3. What should guide you when starting a home-based business?
   - a. A good business idea
   - b. The need to balance business and private obligations
   - c. The desire to involve family members in the business and share business tasks
   - d. By reducing the costs of starting a business (there is no investment in the lease of premises, transportation costs to work and the like).
   - e. Higher earnings
   - **f. Other:**

4. Have you included other members of your family in your regular business activities at home?
   - a. Yes
   - b. No

c. No, since they are not interested in getting involved in my business
d. They do not have the competencies for the business I am running
e. They only have an advisory role and support me
f. Other:

5. What are the basic rules for running a successful home-based business? (circle the three most important)
    a. Required previous experience and professional competencies for the business to be established and developed
    b. Good marketing
    c. Initial capital
    d. Good technical and technological equipment
    e. Workspace
    f. Other:

6. How do you determine if your home-based business is on the right track to success?
    a.) Higher income from expenditures
    b. regularly paid bills
    c. Tax liabilities to the state are paid regularly
    d. External associates are paid regularly
    e. Constant investment in business expansion
    f. Other:

7. How and under what conditions should an office be formed at home?
    a. It is necessary to separate a special area within the home and make it the office
    b. The office should be equipped in the same way as in any other company
    c. Ergonomic rules should be observed when purchasing a desk and other office equipment
    d. A peaceful area should be provided without the possibility of disturbance from the side
    e. Whoever wants to work does not need special conditions
    f) Other:

8. How should you look and be dressed do business at home?
    a. The wardrobe should be adapted to the type of work
    b. One should look the same as when going to the office outside the house

    c. There is no need to get specially dressed up for doing business from home, which is a great advantage of this way of working

    e. It is not very important how we look, but how well we work and complete our obligations

    e. I do not know

    f. Other:

9. Should I be engaged full-time or part-time?

    a. Full-time

    b. Supplementary working time

    c. It depends on whether we already have another job

    d. This is a job without working hours

    e. I do not know

10. Are you one of those owners who believe that their business will increase from year to year and consequently their earnings?

    a. Yes

    b. No

    c. The corona crisis has changed my expectations and reduced my optimism

    e. My business is currently in crisis and I cannot give long-term forecasts

    e. I do not know

    f. Other:

11. What strategies do you use to increase earnings?

    a. I have no specific strategy

    b. I engage valuable associates who know the job well

    c. I rely on expert advice

    d. I constantly follow the professional literature and get additional education

    e. I exchange experiences with other colleagues from the same branch

    f. Other:

12. The most common problems in running a home-based business?

    a. It is difficult to separate business from private obligations

    b. Excessive work, i.e., until the job is done

    c. Lack of social communication

    d. Monotony in doing work, which leads to depression

    e. No special problems

    f. Other:

13. What strategies do you use to overcome them?
    a. I don't know what could be done, but the alienation is great
    b. I set aside one day a week to meet with the external associ-
       ates
    c. I go to meetings and seminars occasionally
    d. I celebrate every success of the company with associates and
       family
    e. I occasionally consult and seek the advice of a psychologist
    f. Other:

14. What are your practical tips as a home business owner to future
    entrepreneurs
    a. Constantly advertise and make your business recognizable
    b. Constantly improve your skills
    c. Try to look representative, which should represent you and
       your business in public
    d. Make a good business plan and learn to manage your time
    e. Always consult with professionals for every aspect of your
       business, thus reducing business risk
    f. Other:

APPENDIX II

Questionnaire for the Economic Part: Employment in the "Gig Economy" in Montenegro

Note: The questions relate to the work of freelancers who work across platforms, connecting them with employers and other workers from around the world. The time and place of work are not important, jobs are project-oriented and carried out under the contract.

Personal data of respondents:

- **Gender**
  a. Male
  b. Female
- **Age**
  a. Less than 24
  b. 25–34
  c. 35–44
  d. 45–54
  e. Above 55
- **Level of Education**
  a. Secondary school
  b. Higher education

Macroeconomics of Western Balkans in the Context of the Global Work and Business Environment, pp. 161–164
Copyright © 2022 by Information Age Publishing
www.infoagepub.com

    c. Master
    d. Doctorate

Questions

1. **Information technologies in the future will enable new employ-ment models**
   a. Yes
   b. No
   c. I do not know

2. **Have you heard about the "Gig Economy" and work across plat-forms?**
   a. Yes
   b. No
   c. Yes, I have, but I'm not familiar

3. **What is important to you when choosing a job?**
   a. Flexible working hours
   b. Opportunity to earn well
   c. Opportunity to acquire new knowledge and advance in the profession.

4. **Would you work in the "Gig Economy" as the only source of income?**
   a. Yes
   b. No
   c. Only if I can't find another job

5. **If you already work in the "Gig Economy," is that your only job and source of income?**
   a. Yes
   b. No
   c. I do it out of a hobby and as a volunteer

6. **Would you change your full-time employment for a flexible con-tract job?**
   a. Yes
   b. No
   c. I just want a secure job

7. **In the last two years, how many employers have you worked for?**
   a. One

b. Between 2 and 5
c. More than 5
d. I do not know

8. **In the last two years, which of the following types of jobs have you done in "Gig Economy?" Select all that applies to you.**
   a. Programming
   b. Teaching
   c. Translation
   d. Research
   e. Other

9. **Do you have access to any of the following benefits offered to you by the job across the platform? Select all that pertains to your job.**
   a. health insurance
   b. life insurance
   c. pension insurance
   d. None of the above

10. **How has your participation in the Gig Economy negatively affected your life?**
    a. Privately
    b. Professionally
    c. Financially
    d. Other

11. **1How has your participation in the Gig Economy positively affected your life?**
    a. Privately
    b. Professionally
    c. Financially
    d. Other

12. **Can working in the "Gig Economy" significantly reduce unemployment?**
    a. Yes
    b. No
    c. I do not know

13. **Can working in the "Gig Economy" contribute to the quality of life of people?**
    a. Yes
    b. No
    c. I do not know

14. How to improve the position of workers working in the "Gig Economy?"
   a. Through the adoption of laws regulating working in this way
   b. Through gaining the trust of freelancers with the employer, which will affect the extension of the employment contract
   c. Through the establishment of a trade union that will fight for the protection of the rights of freelancers

15. Can working across platforms and in the "Gig Economy" reduce the brain drain abroad?
   a. Yes
   b. No
   c. I do not know

APPENDIX III

Questionnaire for the Sociopsychological Part: Working From Home by Countries (Montenegro, B&H, Serbia, and North Macedonia)

The next segment consists of 14 statements. For each of them, indicate how much you agree that it applies to you personally. The degrees of agreement are expressed as follows:

I totally disagree 1
I somewhat disagree...... 2
Neither agree nor disagree 3
I somewhat agree............ 4
I totally agree 5

You need to answer only one of the statements with YES or NO to whether it applies to you.

1. Since I started my own business, I have a lot less time for myself and my hobbies.
2. Working from home does not prevent me from devoting enough time and motivation to engage in physical activities (exercise/sports).

Macroeconomics of Western Balkans in the Context of the Global Work and Business Environment, pp. 165–166
Copyright © 2022 by Information Age Publishing
www.infoagepub.com
165

3. Working from home has negatively affected the amount and quality of sleep.
4. Since I work from home, I pay less attention to my family or partner.
5. Since I work from home, I have more time to hang out with friends.
6. The job I am currently running fulfills me.
7. The current income I earn is enough to cover all my basic needs.
8. I am confident in the future success of the business I am currently running.
9. I have trouble separating my job from my private life
10. Is your work space separate from the space where you spend your free time or sleep (separate room, or bedroom, living room, etc.). Yes/No.
11. I would like to have more contact with other people during my work.
12. Since I work from home, I feel more tense and upset.
13. My family and close friends mostly support me in my current job.
14. During work from home, others (family, friends, neighbors) do not disturb me, and I can fully dedicate myself to work.

ABOUT THE AUTHORS

 **Mirjana Radović-Marković** gained complete expert education from the Faculty of Economics, Belgrade University. She was elected to the position of full professor in a number of universities world-wide. Also, she is a principal research fellow in Serbia and Russia.By invitation, she has given a number of lectures abroad. She had presentation during the meeting of OECD experts in Istanbul (Turkey) (March, 2010), and gave a lecture at Said Business School (June, 2010), Oxford University, U.K., Franklin College, Lugano, Switzerland (2011), University St. Kliment Ohridski, Sofia, Bulgaria (2012–present), VUZF University, Sofia, Bulgaria (2014), South Ural State University (2017–present) and UDG, Podgorica, Montenegro (2019–present). She has written 30 books and more than 250 peer journal articles. For her contribution to the science, she is elected fellow (full fellowship) of the European Academy of Sciences and Arts, Salzburg, Austria, 2014; Elected academician (full fellowship) of Bulgarian Academy of Sciences and Arts, Sofia, Bulgaria, 2013; Elected fellow (full fellowship) of the Academia Europea, London, United Kingdom, 2012; Elected fellow (full fellowship) of the World Academy of Art and Science, United States, 2011; Elected academician (full fellowship) of the Euro Mediterranean Academy of Arts and Sciences–EMAAS, Athens, Greece, 2011; Elected fellow of the Royal Society of the Arts in the U.K. (the RSA), London, United Kingdom, 2010 and others.

**Borislav Đjukanović** In 1965 he enrolled in faculty of philosophy (sociology department) and attained degree in sociology in 1967). He is a professor at UDG, Podgorica, Montenegro. Prof. Đjukanović is a member of board for Social Sciences in Academy of Sciences and Arts of Montenegro. Since 2019. He is an academic of Euro Mediterranean Academy of Arts and Sciences–EMAAS, Athens, Greece.

Printed in the United States
by Baker & Taylor Publisher Services